Stories of America

Volume 1: From Columbus to the Alamo

Consisting of original and revised material from *The Child's Story of America* by Charles Morris, originally published in 1901, and additional material contributed by Sonya Shafer.

Stories of America, Volume 1: From Columbus to the Alamo
© 2011, Simply Charlotte Mason

All rights reserved.

ISBN: 978-1-61634-110-7

Published and printed by
Simply Charlotte Mason, LLC
P.O. Box 892
Grayson, Georgia 30017-0892

Printing date: August 6, 2017

Cover design: John Shafer

www.SimplyCharlotteMason.com

Contents

A Talk with the Young Reader about the History of Our Country

If any of the readers of this book should have a chance to take a trip over the vast region of the United States, from the Atlantic to the Pacific Ocean, from the Great Lakes to the Gulf of Mexico, they would see a wonderful display of cities and towns, of factories and farms, and a great multitude of men and women actively at work. They would behold, spread out on every side, one of the busiest and happiest lands the sun shines upon. Here and there, amid the miles on miles of farms, they might see a forest, here and there a wild beast, here and there an Indian, one of the old people of the land; but these would be almost lost in the rich and prosperous scene.

If our young traveler knew nothing of history, he might fancy that it had always been this way, or that it had taken thousands of years for all those cities to be built and those great fields to be cleared and cultivated. Yet if he had been here only three hundred years ago, he would have seen a very different sight. He could not then have gone over the country by railroad, for such a thing had never been thought of. He could not have gone by paved road, for there was not a road of any kind in the whole length and breadth of the land. Nowhere in this vast country would he have seen a city or town; nowhere a plowed field, a farm-house, or a barn; nowhere a horse, cow, or sheep; nowhere a man with a white or a black face. Instead of great cities he would have seen only clusters of rude huts; instead of fertile farms, only vast reaches of forests; instead of tame cattle, only wild and dangerous beasts; instead of white and black men, only red-skinned Indians.

Just think of it! All that we see around us is the work of less than three hundred years! The story of this great work is called the "History of the United States of America." This story you have before you in the book you now hold. It is written for the boys and girls of our land, but many of their fathers and mothers may find it pleasant and useful to read.

There are hundreds who do not have time to read large histories, which try to tell all that has taken place. For those, this little history will be of great service, in showing them how, from a few half-starved settlers on a wild coast, this great nation has grown up. But I need say no more. The book has its own story to tell. I only lay this introduction before you as a handy stepping-stone into the history itself. By its aid you may cross the brook and wander on through the broad land which lies before you.

Chapter 1
Columbus, the Great Sailor

I t was in the year 1492 that a daring sailor, named Christopher Columbus, crossed a wide ocean and came to this new and wonderful land. Since then men have come here by the millions, and the mighty republic of the United States has grown up with its hundreds of towns and cities.

This is what I have set out to tell you about. I am sure you will all be glad to know how this broad and noble land, once the home of the Native Indians, was discovered and made a home for the white people of Europe.

Some of you may have been told that America was really discovered more than four hundred years before Columbus was born. So it was. At that time some of the bold sailors of the northern countries of Europe, who made the stormy ocean their home and loved the roll of the waves, had come to the frozen island of Iceland. And a ship from Iceland had been driven by the winds to a land in the far west which no man had ever seen before. Was this not America?

Soon after, in the year 1000 one of these Northmen, named Leif Ericson, also known as Leif the Lucky, set sail for this new land. There he found wild grapes growing, and from them he named it Vineland. He also called it Wineland the Good.

After him came others, and there was fighting with the Indians, whom they called Skrellings. In the end the Northmen left the country, and before many years all was forgotten about it. And so time went on for nearly five hundred years more, and nothing was known in Europe about the land beyond the seas.

Now let us go from the north to the south of Europe. Here there is a kingdom called Italy, which runs down into the Mediterranean Sea almost in the shape of a boot. On the western shore of this kingdom is a famous old city named Genoa, in which many daring sailors have dwelt; and here, long ago, lived a man named Columbus, a poor man, who made his living by carding wool.

This poor wool-carder had four children, one of whom (born about 1436) he named Christopher. Almost everybody who has been at school in the world knows the name of this little Italian boy, for he became one of the most famous of men.

Many a boy in our times has to help his father in his shop. The great Benjamin Franklin began work by pouring melted tallow into molds to make candles. In the same way little Columbus had to comb wool for his father, and very likely he got as tired of wool as Franklin did of candles.

The city he lived in was full of sailors, and no doubt he talked to many of them about life on the wild waters, and heard so many stories of danger and adventure that he took the fancy to go to sea himself.

At any rate we are told that he became a sailor when only fourteen years old, and made long and daring voyages while he was still young. Some of those were in Portuguese ships down the coast of Africa, of which continent very little was known at that time. He went north, too; some think as far as Iceland. Who knows but what he was told there of what the Northmen had done?

Columbus spent some time in the island of Madeira, far out in the Atlantic ocean, and there the people told him of strange things they had seen. These had come over the seas before the west winds and floated on their island shores. Among them were pieces of carved wood, and canes so long that they would hold four quarts of wine between their joints. And the dead bodies of two men had also come ashore, whose skins were the color of bronze or copper.

These stories set Columbus thinking. He was now a man, and had read many books of travel, and had studied all that was then known of geography. For a time he lived by making maps and charts for ship captains. This was in the city of Lisbon, in Portugal, where he married and settled down and had little boys of his own.

At that time silk and spices and other rich goods were brought from China and India, thousands of miles to the east, by caravans that traveled overland. Columbus thought that by sailing west, over the broad Atlantic, he would come to these far countries, just as a fly may walk around the surface of an orange and come to the place it started from.

The more Columbus thought about this, the more certain he became that he was right. He was so sure of it that he set out to try and make other people think the same way. He wanted ships with which to sail across the unknown seas to the west, but he had no money of his own to buy them with.

Ah! what a task poor Columbus now had. For years and years he wandered about among the kings and princes of Europe, but no one would believe his story, and many laughed at him and mocked him.

First he tried Genoa, the city where he was born, but the people there told him he was a fool or had lost his senses.

Then he went to the king of Portugal. This king was a rascal and tried to cheat him. He got his plans from him and sent out a vessel in secret, hoping to get the honor of the discovery for himself. But the captain he sent was a coward and was scared by the rolling waves. He soon came back and told the king that there was nothing to be found but water and storm. King John of Portugal was very sorry afterward that he had tried to rob Columbus of his honor.

Columbus was very angry when he heard what the king had done. He left Portugal for Spain and tried to get the king and queen of that country to let him have ships and sailors. But they were at war with a people called the Moors and had no money to spare for anything but fighting and killing.

Columbus stayed there for seven long years. After these many years Columbus got tired of trying in Spain. He now set out for France to see what the king of that country would do. He sent one of his brothers to England to see its king and ask him for aid.

He was now so poor that he had to travel along the dusty roads on foot, his little son going with him. One day he stopped at a convent called La Rabida to beg some bread for his son, who was very hungry.

The good monks gave bread to the boy, and while he was eating it the prior of the convent came out and talked with Columbus, asking him his business. Columbus told him his story. He told it so well that the prior believed in it. He asked him to stay there with his son and said he would write to Isabella, the queen of Spain, whom he knew very well.

So Columbus stayed, and the prior wrote a letter to the queen, and in the end the wandering sailor was sent for to come back to the king's court.

Queen Isabella deserves much of the honor of the discovery of America. The king would not listen to the wandering sailor, but the queen offered to pledge her jewels to raise money which he needed for ships and sailors.

Columbus had won. After years and years of toil and hunger and disappointment, he was to have ships and sailors and supplies and to be given a chance to prove whether he was a fool or not.

But such ships as they gave him! Why, you can see far better ones every day, sailing down your rivers. Two of them did not even have decks, but were like open boats. With this small fleet Columbus set sail from Palos, a little port in Spain, on the third of August, 1492, on one of the most wonderful voyages that has ever been known.

Away they went far out into the "Sea of Darkness," as the

Atlantic ocean was then called. Mile after mile, league after league, day after day, on and on they went, seeing nothing but the endless waves, while the wind drove them steadily into the unknown west.

The sailors never expected to see their wives and children again. They were frightened when they started, and every day they grew more scared. They looked with staring eyes for the bleak fogs or the frightful monsters of which they had been told. At one place they came upon great tracts of seaweed and thought they were in shallow water and would be wrecked on banks of mud. Then the compass, to which they trusted, ceased to point due north and they were more frightened than ever. Soon there was hardly a stout heart in the fleet except that of Columbus.

The time came when the sailors grew half mad with fear. Some of them made a plot to throw Columbus overboard and sail home again. They would tell the people there that he had fallen into the sea and been drowned.

It was a terrible thing to do, was it not? But desperate men will do dreadful things. They thought one man had better die than all of them. Only a happy discovery saved the life of the great navigator.

One day a glad sailor called his comrades and pointed over the side. A branch of a green bush was floating by with fresh berries on it. It looked as if it had just been broken off a bush. Another day one of them picked from the water a stick which had been carved with a knife. Land birds were seen flying over the ships. Hope came back to their hearts. They were sure now that land must be near.

October 11th came. When night fell dozens of men were on the look-out. Each wanted to be the first to see land. About 10:00 that night, Columbus, who was looking out over the waves, saw a light far off. It moved up and down like a lantern carried in a man's hand.

Hope now grew strong. Every eye looked out into the darkness.

About 2:00 in the morning came the glad cry of "Land! Land!" A gun was fired from the leading vessel. One of its sailors had seen what looked like land in the moonlight. You may be sure no one slept any more that night.

When daylight came the joyful sailors saw before them a low, green shore, on which the sunlight lay in beauty; men and women stood on it, looking in wonder at the ships, which they thought must be great white-winged birds. They had never seen such things before. We can hardly imagine what we would have done under similar circumstances.

When the boats from the ships came to the shore, and Columbus landed, clad in shining armor and bearing the great banner of Spain, the simple natives fell to the ground on their faces. They thought the gods had come from heaven to visit them.

Some of the red-skinned natives wore ornaments of gold. They were asked by signs where they had got this gold, and pointed south. Soon all were on board again, the ships once more spread their sails, and swiftly they flew southward before the wind.

Day by day, as they went on, new islands arose, some small, some large, all green and beautiful. Columbus thought this must be India, which he had set out to find, and he called the people Indians. He never knew that it was a new continent he had discovered.

The month of March of the next year came before the little fleet sailed again into the port of Palos. The people hailed it with shouts of joy, for they had mourned their friends as dead.

Fast spread the news. When Columbus entered Barcelona, where the king and queen were, bringing with him new plants, birds, and animals, strange weapons, golden ornaments, and some of the red-skinned natives, he was received as if he had been a king. He was seated beside the king; he rode by his side in the street; he was made a grandee of Spain; all the honors of the kingdom were showered on him.

We here recall the incident of Columbus and the egg. A dinner was given in his honor and many great men were there. The attention Columbus received made some people jealous. One of them with a sneer asked Columbus if he did not think any one else could have discovered the Indies. In answer Columbus took an egg from a dish on the table and, handing it to the questioner, asked him to make it stand on end.

After trying several times, the man gave it up. Columbus, taking the egg in his hand, tapping it gently on one end against the top of the table so as to break the shell slightly, made it balance.

"Any one could do that," said the man.

"So any one can discover the Indies after I have shown him the way," said Columbus.

It was his day of pride and triumph. Poor Columbus was soon to find out how Spain treated its benefactors. Three times again he sailed to the New World, and once a base Spanish governor sent him back to Spain with chains upon his limbs. Those chains he kept hanging in his room till he died, and asked that they should be buried with him.

They who had once given him every honor, now treated him with shameful neglect. He who had ridden beside the king and dined with the highest nobles of Spain, became poor, sad, and lonely.

He died in 1506, fourteen years after his great discovery. Then Spain, which had treated him so badly, began to honor his memory. But it came too late for poor Columbus, who had been allowed to die almost like a pauper, after he had made Spain the richest country in Europe.

Columbus

by Joaquin Miller

Behind him lay the gray Azores,
 Behind the Gates of Hercules;
Before him not the ghost of shores,
 Before him only shoreless seas.
The good mate said: "Now must we pray,
 For lo! the very stars are gone.
Brave Admiral, speak, what shall I say?"
 "Why, say, 'Sail on! sail on! and on!'"

"My men grow mutinous day by day;
 My men grow ghastly wan and weak."
The stout mate thought of home; a spray
 Of salt wave washed his swarthy cheek.
"What shall I say, brave Admiral, say,
 If we sight naught but seas at dawn?"
"Why, you shall say at break of day,
 'Sail on! sail on! sail on! and on!"

They sailed and sailed, as winds might blow,
 Until at last the blanched mate said:
"Why, now not even God would know
 Should I and all my men fall dead.
These very winds forget their way,
 For God from these dread seas is gone.

Now speak, brave Admiral, speak and say"—
    He said: "Sail on! sail on! and on!"

They sailed. They sailed. Then spake the mate:
    "This mad sea shows his teeth to-night.
He curls his lip, he lies in wait,
    With lifted teeth, as if to bite!
Brave Admiral, say but one good word:
    What shall we do when hope is gone?"
The words leapt like a leaping sword:
    "Sail on! sail on! sail on! and on!"

Then, pale and worn, he kept his deck,
    And peered through darkness. Ah, that night
Of all dark nights! And then a speck—
    A light! A light! A light! A light!
It grew, a starlit flag unfurled!
    It grew to be Time's burst of dawn.
He gained a world; he gave that world
    Its grandest lesson: "On! sail on!"

Chapter 2
Captain John Smith and Jamestown

The English were in no hurry in sending out settlers to the New World which Columbus had discovered. While the Spaniards were seeking gold and empires in the south, and the French were catching fish and exploring the rivers and lakes in the north, all the English did was to rob the Spanish ships and settlements and to bring them slaves from Africa.

But the time came, a hundred years after America was discovered, when some of the English tried to form a settlement on the coast of North Carolina. Poor settlers! When the next ship came out, they were all gone. Not a soul of them could be found. Nothing was left but some letters they had cut into the bark of a tree. What became of them nobody ever knew.

Nothing more was done until the year 1607, when the ship in which Captain John Smith had taken passage sailed up a bright and beautiful river in Virginia. What do you think of Captain John Smith, the hero of Virginia? Was he not a man to dream of, a true hero of romance? Why, I feel half ashamed to say anything about him, for every one of you must know his story. I am sure all those who love romance have read about him.

John Smith was not the kind of man to work at a trade. He ran away from home when a boy and became a wanderer over the earth. And a hard life he had of it. At one place he was robbed, and at another place was shipwrecked. Once he leaped overboard from a ship and swam ashore. Once again he fought with three Turks and killed all of them without help. Then he was taken prisoner and sold as a slave to a cruel Turk, who put a ring round his neck and made him work very hard.

One day his master came out where he was at work and struck him with his whip. He soon found that John Smith was a bad man to whip. He hit the Turk a hard blow with the flail he was using, and killed him on the spot. Then he ran away, got to Russia, and in time, made his way back to England. But England was too quiet a place for him. A ship was about to cross the sea to America and he volunteered to go in it. He had not half enough of adventure yet. Some people think that Captain Smith bragged a little and did not do all he said. Well, that may be so. But it is certain that he was a brave and bold man, and just the man to help settle a new country.

It was the month of May, and the banks were covered with flowers when the ship Smith was on arrived in America. The colonists thought this a very good place to live in, so they landed and began to look around them. The river they called the James, and the place they named Jamestown. But instead of building a town and preparing for the future, as sensible men would have done, they began to seek for gold, and soon they were in no end of trouble. In a short time their food was all eaten. Then some of them took sick and died. Others were killed by Indians. It looked as if this colony would come to grief as did the former one.

So it would if it had not been for Captain Smith. He was only one man among a hundred, but he was worth more than all the rest of the hundred. He could not keep still, but hustled about, here, there, and everywhere. Now he was exploring the country, sailing up the rivers or up the broad Chesapeake Bay. Now he was talking with the Indians, getting food from them for the starving colonists. Now he was doing his best to make the men build houses and dig and plant the ground. You can see that John Smith had enough to keep him busy. He had many adventures with the Indians. At one time he was taken prisoner by them and was in terrible danger of being killed. But he showed them his pocket compass, and when they saw the needle always pointing north, they thought there must be magic in it. They were still more surprised when he sent one of them with a letter to his friends. They did not understand how a piece of paper could talk, as his paper seemed to do.

But all this was not enough to save his life. The great chief Powhatan looked on him as the leader of these white strangers who had settled in his land. He wanted to get rid of them, and thought that if he killed the man of the magic needle and the talking paper they would certainly be scared and go away.

So Captain Smith was tied hand and foot and lain on the ground with his head on a log. And a powerful Indian stood near by with a great war club in his hand. Only a sign from Powhatan was needed, and down would come that club on the white man's head and it would be all over with the brave and bold John Smith.

Alas! poor Captain Smith! There was no pity in Powhatan's eyes.The burly Indian twisted his fingers about the club and lifted it in the air. One minute more and it might be all over with the man who had killed three Turks in one fight. But before that minute was over, a strange thing took place. A young Indian girl came running wildly into the hut, with her hair flying and her eyes wet with tears. And she flung herself on the ground and laid her head on that of the bound prisoner, and begged the chief to give him his life.

It was Pocahontas, the pretty young daughter of Powhatan. She pleaded so pitifully that the chief's heart was touched, and he consented that the captive should live, and bade them take the bonds from his limbs.

Do you not think this a very pretty story? Some say that it is not true, but I think very likely it is. At any rate, it is so pretty that it ought to be true. Afterwards this interesting Indian Princess married one of the Virginians named John Rolfe and was taken to London and presented to the Queen.

Captain Smith got safe back to Jamestown. But his troubles

were not at an end, for the colonists were as hard to deal with as the Indians. Some of them had found a kind of yellow stuff which they were sure was gold. They loaded a ship with this and sent it to England, thinking that they would all be rich. But the yellow stuff proved to be what is known as "fools' gold," and worth no more than so much sand. Instead of becoming rich, they were laughed at as great fools.

After a while Smith was made governor, and he now tried a new plan to make the men work. He told them that if they did not work they should not eat. None of them wanted to starve, and they knew that John Smith meant just what he said, so they began to build houses and to dig the ground and plant crops. But some of them grumbled and some of them swore, and it was anything but a happy family.

Captain Smith did not like this swearing, and he took a funny way to stop it. When the men came home at night, each one who had sworn had a can of cold water poured down his sleeve for every time he had done so. Did any of my readers ever try that? If they did they would know why the men soon quit grumbling and swearing. All was beginning to do well in the colony when Captain Smith was hurt by some gunpowder that took fire and went off. He was hurt so badly that he had to go back to England. After that all went ill.

As soon as their governor was gone, the lazy men quit working. The profane men swore worse than before. They ate up all their food in a hurry, and the Indians would bring them no more. Sickness and hunger came and carried many of them to the grave. Some of them meddled with the Indians and were killed. There were five hundred of them when winter set in; but when spring came only sixty of them were alive. And all this took place because one wise man, Captain John Smith, was hurt and had to go home.

The whole colony would have broken up if ships had not come out with more men and plenty of food. Soon after that, the people began to plant the ground and raise tobacco, which sold well in England. Many of them became rich, and the little settlement at Jamestown, in time, grew into the great colony of Virginia.

Pocahontas

William Makepeace Thackeray

Wearied arm and broken sword
 Wage in vain the desperate fight:
Round him press a countless horde,
 He is but a single knight.
Hark! a cry of triumph shrill
 Through the wilderness resounds,
As, with twenty bleeding wounds,
 Sinks the warrior, fighting still.
Now they heap the funeral pyre,
 And the torch of death they light:
Ah! 'tis hard to die by fire!
 Who will shield the captive knight?
Round the stake with fiendish cry
 Wheel and dance the savage crowd,
Cold the victim's mien and proud.
 And his breast is bared to die.
Who will shield the fearless heart?
 Who avert the murderous blade?
From the throng with sudden start
 See, there springs an Indian maid.
Quick she stands before the knight:
 "Loose the chain, unbind the ring,
I am daughter of the king,
 And I claim the Indian right!"

Dauntlessly aside she flings
  Lifted axe and thirsty knife,
Fondly to his heart she clings,
  And her bosom guards his life!
In the woods of Powhatan,
  Still 'tis told by Indian fires
How a daughter of their sires
  Saved the captive Englishman.

Chapter 3
Captain Miles Standish and the Pilgrims

In the year 1620, thirteen years after Smith and his fellows sailed up the James River, a shipload of men and women came to a place called Plymouth, on the rocky coast of New England. It was named Plymouth by Captain Smith, who had been there before.

These people are known as Pilgrims. They had been badly treated at home because they did not believe in the doctrines of the Church of England, and they had come across the stormy sea to find a place where they could worship God in their own way, without fear of being put in prison.

With them came a soldier. He was named Captain Miles Standish. He was a little man, but he carried a big sword and had a stout heart and a hot temper. While the Pilgrims came to work and to pray, Captain Standish came to fight. He was a different man from Captain Smith and would not have been able to deal with the lazy folks at Jamestown. But the Pilgrims were different also. They expected to work and live by their labor, and they had no sooner landed on Plymouth Rock than they began to dig and plant, while the sound of the hammer rang merrily all day long as they built houses and got ready for the cold winter. But for all their labor and carefulness, sickness and hunger came, as they had done at Jamestown, and by the time spring came, half the poor Pilgrims were dead.

The Indians soon got to be afraid of Captain Standish. They were afraid of the Pilgrims, too, for they found that these religious men could fight as well as pray. One Indian chief, named Canonicus, sent them a bundle of arrows with a snake's skin tied round it. This was their way of saying that they were going to fight the Pilgrims and drive them from the country. But Governor Bradford filled the snake skin with powder and bullets and sent it back. When Canonicus saw this, he was badly scared, for he knew well what it meant. He had heard the white men's guns and thought they had the power of using thunder and lightning. So he made up his mind to let the white strangers alone.

But the Pilgrims did not trust the Indians. They put cannon on the roof of their log church, and they walked to church on Sunday like so many soldiers on the march, with guns in their hands and Captain Standish at their head. And while they were listening to the sermon, one man stood outside on the lookout for danger.

At one time some of the Indians made a plot to kill all the English. A friendly Indian told Captain Standish about it, and he made up his mind to teach them a lesson they would remember. He went to the Indian camp with a few men and walked boldly into the hut where the plotting chiefs were talking over their plans. When they saw him and the men with him, they tried to frighten them. One of them showed the Captain his knife and talked very boldly about it.

A big Indian looked with scorn on the little Captain. "Poh, you are only a little fellow, if you are a captain," he said. "I am not a chief, but I am strong and brave."

Captain Standish was very angry, but he said nothing then. He waited until the next day, when he met the chiefs again. Then there was a quarrel and a fight, and the little captain killed the big Indian with his own knife. More of the Indians were slain, and the others ran for the woods. That put an end to the plot.

There is one funny story told about Captain Standish. His wife had died, and he felt so lonely that he wanted another. So he picked out a pretty young woman named Priscilla Mullins. But the rough old soldier knew more about fighting than about talking to women, and he sent his young friend, John Alden, to speak for him.

John told Priscilla's father what he had come for, and the father told Priscilla what John had told him. The pretty Priscilla had no fancy for the wrinkled old soldier. She looked at her father. Then she looked at John. Then she said, "Why don't you speak for yourself, John?"

John did speak for himself, and Priscilla became his wife. As for the captain, he married another woman, and this time I fancy he "spoke for himself."

Miles Standish lived to be 70 years old and to have a farm of his own and a house on a high hill near Plymouth. It is called Captain's Hill.

The Landing of the Pilgrim Fathers

Felicia Dorothea Hemans

The breaking waves dashed high
On a stern and rock-bound coast,
And the woods, against a stormy sky,
Their giant branches tossed;

And the heavy night hung dark
The hills and waters o'er,
When a band of exiles moored their bark
On the wild New England shore.

Not as the conqueror comes,
They, the true-hearted, came;
Not with the roll of the stirring drums,
And the trumpet that sings of fame;

Not as the flying come,
In silence and in fear;—
They shook the depths of the desert's gloom
With their hymns of lofty cheer.

Amidst the storm they sang,
And the stars heard, and the sea;
And the sounding aisles of the dim woods rang
To the anthem of the free!

The ocean-eagle soared
From his nest by the white wave's foam,
And the rocking pines of the forest roared;
This was their welcome home!

There were men with hoary hair
Amidst that pilgrim band;
Why had they come to wither there,
Away from their childhood's land?

There was woman's fearless eye,
Lit by her deep love's truth;
There was manhood's brow, serenely high,
And the fiery heart of youth.

What sought they thus afar?
Bright jewels of the mine?
The wealth of seas, the spoils of war?—
They sought a faith's pure shrine!

Ay, call it holy ground,
The soil where first they trod!
They left unstained what there they found—
Freedom to worship God!

Chapter 4

Roger Williams
and the Puritans

We have now another hero to speak of, Roger Williams. He was not a captain like John Smith or Miles Standish. He was a preacher. But he was a brave man and showed in his way as much courage as either of the captains.

The Pilgrims were quickly followed by other people, who settled at Boston and other places around Massachusetts Bay until there were a great many of them. These were called Puritans. They came across the seas for the same reason as the Pilgrims, to worship God in their own way.

But they were as hard to live with as the people at home, for they wanted to force everybody else into their way. Some Quakers who came to Boston were treated very badly because they had different beliefs from the Puritans. And one young minister named Roger Williams, who thought every man should have the right to worship as he pleased, and said that the Indians had not been treated justly, had to flee into the woods for safety.

It was winter time. The trees were bare of leaves and the ground was white with snow. Poor Roger had to wander through the cold woods, making a fire at night with his flint and steel, or sometimes creeping into a hollow tree to sleep.

Thus he went on, half frozen and half starved, for eighty long miles to the house of Massasoit, an Indian chief who was his friend. The good chief treated him well, for he knew, like all the Indians, what Roger Williams had tried to do for them. When spring time came, Massasoit gave his guest a canoe and told him where to go. So Roger paddled away till he found a good place to stop. This place he called Providence. A large city now stands there, and is still called Providence.

Roger Williams had some friends with him, and others soon came, and after a few years he had quite a colony of his own. It was called Rhode Island.

He took care that the Indians should be treated well, and that no one should do them any harm, so they grew to love the good white man. And he said that every man in his colony should have what religion he liked best, and no one should suffer on account of his mode of worship.

It was a wonderful thing in those days, when there were wars going on in Europe about religion, and everybody was punished who did not believe in the religion of the state.

Do you not think that Roger Williams was as brave a man as John Smith or Miles Standish, and as much of a hero? He did not kill any one. He was not that kind of a hero. But he did much to make men happy and good and to do justice to all men, and I think that is the best kind of a hero.

The New England Primer
Alphabet 1727

In Adam's fall
We sinned all.

Thy life to mend
This Book attend.

The Cat doth play
And after slay.

A Dog will bite
A thief at night.

An Eagle's flight
Is out of sight.

The idle Fool
Is whipped at school.

As runs the Glass
Man's life doth pass.

My book and Heart
Shall never part.

Job feels the rod
Yet blesses God.

Our King the good
No man of blood.

The Lion bold
The Lamb doth hold.

The Moon gives light
In time of night.

Nightingales sing
In time of spring.

The royal Oak was the tree
That saved his Royal Majesty.

Peter denies
His Lord and cries.

Queen Esther comes in Royal State
To save the Jews from dismal fate.

Rachel does mourn
For her firstborn.

Samuel anoints
Whom God appoints.

Time cuts down all
Both great and small.

Uriah's beauteous wife
Made David seek his life.

Whales in the sea
God's voice obey.

Xerxes the great did die
And so must you and I.

Youth forward slips.
Death soonest nips.

Zaccheus he
Did climb the tree
His Lord to see.

Chapter 5

How the Dutch Came to America

I wonder how many of my readers have ever seen the great city of New York. I wonder still more how many of them know that it is one of the largest cities in the world. Yet it has not been around so very long.

Why, if you should go back no farther than the time of your great-great-great-grandfather you would find no city of New York. All you would see would be a sort of large village on Manhattan Island, at the mouth of the Hudson River. And if you went back to the time of your grandfather's great-great-grandfather, I fancy you would see nothing on that island but trees with Indian wigwams beneath them. Not a single white man or a single house would you see.

In the year 1609, just two years after Captain Smith sailed into the James River, a queer-looking Dutch vessel came across the ocean and began to prowl up and down the coast. It was named the "Half Moon." It came from Holland, the land of the Dutch, but its captain was an English man named Henry Hudson, who had done so many daring things that men called him "the bold Englishman."

What Captain Hudson would have liked to do was to sail across the United States and come out into the Pacific Ocean, and so make his way to the rich countries of Asia. Was not that a funny notion? To think that he could sail across three thousand miles of land and across great ranges of mountains!

But you must not think that Captain Hudson was crazy. Nobody then knew how wide America was. For all they knew it might not be fifty miles wide. Captain John Smith tried to get across it by sailing up James River. And Captain Hudson fancied he might find some stream that led from one ocean to the other.

So on he went up and down the coast, looking for an opening. And after a while the "Half Moon" sailed into a broad and beautiful bay, where great trees came down to the edge of the water and Indians paddled about in their canoes. Captain Hudson was delighted to see it. "It was," he said, "as pleasant with grass and flowers as he had ever seen, and very sweet smells."

This body of water was what we now call New York Bay. A broad and swift river runs into it, which is now called Hudson River, after Henry Hudson. The bold captain thought that this was the stream to go up if he wished to reach the Pacific Ocean. So, after talking as well as he could with the Indians in their canoes and trading beads for corn, he set his sails again and started up the splendid river. Some of the Indians came on board the "Half Moon," and the Dutch gave them brandy, which they had never seen or tasted before. Soon they were dancing and capering about the deck, and one of them fell down so stupid with drink that his friends thought he was dead. This was their first taste of the deadly "fire water" of the whites, which has killed thousands of Indians since then.

Captain Hudson and the Dutch no doubt thought that this was great fun. People often do much harm without stopping to think. But on up the river went the "Half Moon."

At some places they saw fields of green corn on the water's edge. Farther on were groves of lofty trees, and for miles great cliffs of rock rose like towers. It was all very grand and beautiful.

"It was a very good land to fall in with," said Captain Hudson, "and a pleasant land to see."

They sailed on and on till they came to mountains, which rose on both sides of the river. After passing the mountains, the captain went ashore to visit an old chief, who lived in a round house built of bark. The Indians here had great heaps of corn and beans. But what they liked best was roast dog. They roasted a dog for Captain Hudson and asked him to eat it, but I do not know whether he did so or not. And they broke their arrows and threw them into the fire, to show that they did not mean to do harm to the white men.

After leaving the good old chief, the Dutch explorers went on up the river till they reached a place about 150 miles above the sea, where the city of Albany now stands. Here the river became so narrow and shallow that Captain Hudson saw he could not reach the Pacific by that route, so he turned and sailed back to the sea again.

A sad fate was that of Captain Hudson, "the bold Englishman." The next year he came back to America. But this time he went far to the north and entered the great body of water which we call Hudson Bay. He thought this would lead to the Pacific, and he would not turn back, though the food was nearly all gone. At last the crew got desperate, and they put the captain and some others into an open boat on the wide waters and turned back again. Nothing more was ever heard of Captain Hudson, and he must have died miserably on that cold and lonely bay.

But he had told the Dutch people all about Hudson River, and that the Indians had many fine furs, which they would be glad to trade for beads and knives and other cheap things. The Dutch were fond of trading and liked to make a good bargain, so they soon began to send ships to America. They built a fort and some log huts on Manhattan Island, and a number of them stayed there to trade with the Indians. They paid the Indians for the island with some cheap goods worth about twenty-four dollars. I do not think any of you could guess the great city of New York stands where the log huts of the Dutch traders once stood, and twenty-four dollars would hardly buy as much land as you could cover with your hand.

The country around is now all farming land, where grain and fruit are grown and cattle are raised. But then it was all woodland for hundreds of miles away, and in these woods lived many foxes and beavers and other fur-bearing animals. These the Indians hunted and killed and sold their furs to the Dutch, so that there was soon a good trade for both the Indians and the white men. The Dutch were glad to get the furs, and the Indians were as glad to get the knives and beads. More and more people came from Holland, and the town grew larger and larger, and strong brick houses took the place of the log huts, and in time, there was quite a town.

Men were sent from Holland to govern the people. Some of these men were not fit to govern themselves, and the settlers did not like to have such men over them. One of them was a stubborn old fellow named Peter Stuyvesant. He had lost one of his legs and wore a wooden leg with bands of silver round it, so that he was called "Old Silver Leg."

While he was governor an important event took place. The English had a settlement in Virginia and another in New England, and they said that all the coast lands belonged to them, because the Cabots had been the first to see them. The Cabots came from Italy, but they had settled in England and sailed in an English ship.

So one day a small fleet of English vessels came into the bay, and a letter was sent on shore which said that all this land belonged to England and must be given up to them. The Dutch might stay there, but they would be under an English governor. Old Peter tore up the letter and stamped about in a great rage on his silver leg. But he had treated the people so badly that they would not fight for him, so he had to give up the town.

The English called it New York, after the Duke of York, the king's brother. It grew and grew till it got to be a great and rich city and sent ships to all parts of the world. Most of the Dutch stayed there, and their descendants are among the best people of New York today.

www.SimplyCharlotteMason.com

Chapter 6
How the Quakers Came to America

N ot long after these English ships came to New York Bay, other English ships came to a fine body of water, about 100 miles farther south, now called Delaware Bay. Into this also runs a great stream of fresh water, called Delaware River, as wide as the Hudson. I think you will like to learn what brought them here.

No doubt you remember what I said about some people called Quakers, who came to Boston and were treated very badly by the Puritans. Did any of my young readers ever see a Quaker? In old times you would have known them, for they dressed in a different way from other people. They wore very plain clothes and broad brimmed hats, which they would not take off to do honor to king or noble. Today they generally dress more like the people around them.

If they were treated badly in Boston, they were treated worse in England. Thieves and highwaymen had as good a time as the poor Quakers. Some of them were put in jail and kept there for years. Some were whipped or put in the stocks, where low people called them vile names and threw mud at them. Indeed, these quiet people, who did no harm to any one but were kind to others, had a very hard time and were treated more cruelly than the Pilgrims and the Puritans.

Among them was the son of a brave English admiral who was

a friend of the king and his brother, the Duke of York. But this did not save him from being put in prison for preaching the Quaker doctrines and wearing his hat in court.

This was William Penn from whom Pennsylvania was named. You may well fancy that the son of a rich admiral and the friend of a king did not like being treated as though he were a thief because he chose to wear a hat with a broad brim and to say "thee" and "thou," and because he would not go to the king's church.

What is more, the king owed him money, which he could not or would not pay. He had owed this money to Admiral Penn, and after the admiral died, he owed it to his son.

William Penn thought it would be wise to do as the Pilgrims and Puritans had done. There was plenty of land in America, and it would be easy there to make a home for the poor Quakers where they could live in peace and worship God in the way they thought right. This they could not do in England.

Penn went to the king and told him how he could pay his debt. If the king would give him a tract of land on the west side of the Delaware River, he would give him a receipt in full for the money owing to his father.

King Charles, who never had money enough for his own use, was very glad to pay his debts in this easy way. He told Penn that he could have all the land he wanted and offered him a tract that was nearly as large as the whole of England. This land belonged to the Indians, but that did not trouble King Charles. It is easy to pay debts in other people's property. All Penn was asked to pay the king was two beaver skins every year and one-fifth of all the gold and silver that should be mined. As no gold or silver was ever mined, the king got nothing but his beaver skins, which were a kind of rent.

What do any of my young readers know about the Delaware River? Have any of you seen the wide, swift stream which flows between the states of Pennsylvania and New Jersey and runs into the broad body of water known as Delaware Bay? On its banks stands the great city of Philadelphia, in which live more than a million people, and where there are thousands of busy workshops and well-filled stores. This large and fine city came from the way the king paid his debt. King Charles was not a good man, but he did one good thing.

There were white men there before the Quakers came. Many years earlier a number of people from Sweden had come and settled along the river. Then the Dutch from New York said the land was theirs and took possession of the forts of the Swedes. Then the English of New York claimed the land as theirs. Then Quakers came and settled in New Jersey. Finally came William Penn, in a ship called by the pretty name of "Welcome," and after that the land belonged to the Quakers or Friends, though the Swedes stayed there still.

We have something very pleasant to say about good William Penn. He knew very well that King Charles did not own the land and had no right to sell it or give it away. So he called the Indians together under a great elm tree on the river bank and had a long talk with them and told them he would pay them for all the land he wanted. This pleased the Indians very much, and ever afterwards they loved William Penn.

Do you not think it must have been a pretty scene when Penn and the Quakers met the Indian chiefs under the great tree—the Indians in their colored blankets and the Quakers in their great hats? That tree stood for more than a hundred years afterwards, and when the British army was in Philadelphia during the war of the Revolution, their general put a guard around Penn's treaty tree so that the soldiers should not cut it down for firewood. The tree is gone now, but a stone monument marks where it stood. A city was laid out on the river, which Penn named Philadelphia, or Brotherly Love. I suppose there is some brotherly love there still, but not nearly so much as there should be.

Streets were made through the woods, and the names of the trees were given to these streets, which are still known as

Chestnut, Walnut, Pine, Cherry, and the like. People soon came in numbers, and it is wonderful how fast the city grew. Soon there were hundreds of comfortable houses, and in time, it got to be the largest city in the country.

The Indians looked on in wonder to see large houses springing up where they had hunted deer and to see great ships where they had paddled their canoes. But the white men spread more and more into the land, and the Indians were pushed back, and in time, none of them were left in Penn's woodland colony. This was long after William Penn was dead.

But while Penn's city was growing large and rich, he was becoming poor. He spent much money on his province and got very little back. At last he became so poor that he was put in prison for debt, as was the custom in those days. In the end he died and left the province to his sons. The Indians sent some beautiful furs to his widow in memory of their great and good brother. They said these were to make her a cloak "to protect her while she was passing without her guide through the stormy wilderness of life."

Chapter 7

Maryland

Virginia has often been called the Cavalier colony. Do any of you know why, or who the Cavaliers were? Perhaps I had better tell you. They were the lords and the proud people of England. Many of them had no money, but they would do no work and cared for nothing but pleasure and fighting. There were plenty of working people in that country, but there were many who were too proud to work and expected others to work for them, while they hoped to live by gambling and cheating.

These were the kind of men who came out with John Smith, and that is why he had so much trouble with them. The Puritans and the Quakers came from the working people of England, and nobody had to starve them to make them work, or to pour cold water down their sleeves to stop them from swearing.

While religious people settled in the North, many of the proud Cavalier class, who cared very little about religion, came to the South. So we may call the southern settlements the Cavalier colonies, though many of the common people came there too, and it was not long before there was plenty of work.

The first to come after John Smith and the Jamestown people were some shiploads of Catholics. You should know that the Catholics were treated in England even worse than the Puritans and the Quakers. The law said they must go to the English Church instead of to their own. If they did not, they would have to pay a large sum of money or go to prison. Was not this very harsh and unjust?

The Catholics were not all poor people. There were rich men and nobles among them. One of these nobles, named Lord Baltimore, asked the King for some land in America where he and his friends might dwell in peace and have churches of their own. This was many years before William Penn asked for the same thing. The King was a friend of Lord Baltimore and told him he might have as much land as he could make use of. So he picked out a large tract just north of Virginia, which the King named Maryland, after his wife, Queen Mary, who was a Catholic. All Lord Baltimore had to pay for this was two Indian arrows every year and a part of the gold and silver, if any were found. This was done to show that the King still kept some claim to Maryland and did not give away all his rights.

And now comes a story much the same as I have told you several times already. A shipload of Catholics and other people came across the ocean to the new continent which Columbus had discovered many years before. These sailed up the broad Chesapeake Bay. You may easily find this bay on your map. They landed at a place they called St. Mary's, where there was a small Indian town. As it happened, the Indians at this town had been so much troubled by fighting tribes farther north that they were just going to move somewhere else. So they were very glad to sell their town to the white strangers.

All they wanted for their houses and their corn fields were some hatchets, knives and beads, and other things they could use. Gold and silver would have been of no value to them, for the only money the Indians used was round pieces of sea-shell with holes bored through them. Before these people left their town, they showed the white men how to hunt in the woods and how to plant corn. And their wives taught the white women how to make hominy out of corn and how to bake johnny-cakes. So the people of Maryland did not suffer from hunger like those of Virginia and

New England, and they had plenty to eat and got along very well from the start.

This was in the year 1634, just about the time Roger Williams went to Rhode Island. Lord Baltimore did the same thing that Roger Williams did; he gave the people religious liberty. Every Christian who came to Maryland had the right to worship God in his own way. Roger Williams went farther than this, for he gave the same right to Jews and all other people, whether they were Christians or not.

It was not long before other people came to Maryland, and they began to plant tobacco, as the people were doing in Virginia. Tobacco was a good crop to raise, for it could be sold for a high price in England, so that the Maryland planters did very well and many of them got to be rich. But religious liberty did not last there very long, and the Catholics were not much better off than they had been in England. All the poor people who came with Lord Baltimore were Protestants. Only the rich ones were Catholics. Many other Protestants soon came, some of them being Puritans from New England, who did not know what religious liberty meant.

These people said that the Catholics should not have the right to worship in their own churches, even in Maryland, and they went so far that they tried to take from Lord Baltimore the lands which the king had given him. There was much fighting between the Catholics and the Protestants. Now one party got the best of it, and now the other. In the end the province was taken from Lord Baltimore's son; and when a new king, named King William, came to the throne, he said that Maryland was his property and that the Catholics should not have a church of their own or worship in their own way in that province. Do you not think this was very cruel and unjust? It seems so to me. It did not seem right, after Lord Baltimore had given religious liberty to all men, for others to come and take it away. But the custom in those days was that all men must be made to think the same way or be punished if they didn't. This seems queer now-a-days, when every man has the right to think as he pleases.

In time there was born a Lord Baltimore who became a Protestant, and the province was given back to him. It grew rich and full of people, and large towns were built. One of these was named Baltimore, after Lord Baltimore, and is now a great city. And Washington, the capital of the United States, stands on land that was once part of Maryland. But St. Mary's, the first town built, has gone, and there is hardly a mark left to show where it stood.

Chapter 8

The Carolinas

Maryland, as I have said, lies north of Virginia. The Potomac River runs between them. South of Virginia was another great tract of land, extending all the way to Florida, which the Spaniards then held. Some French Protestants tried to settle there, but they had been cruelly murdered by the Spaniards, and no one else came there for many years.

About 1660 people began to settle in what was then called "the Carolinas," but is now called North Carolina and South Carolina. Some of these came from Virginia and some from England, and small settlements were made here and there along the coast. One of these was called Charleston. This has now grown into a large and important city.

There were some noblemen in England who thought that this region might become worth much money, so they asked the king, Charles II, to give it to them. This was the same king who gave the Dutch settlement to the Duke of York and who afterwards gave Pennsylvania to William Penn. He was very ready to give away what did not belong to him, and told these noblemen that they were welcome to the Carolinas. There were eight of these men, and they made up their minds that they would have a very nice form of government for their new province. So they went to a celebrated philosopher named John Locke and asked him to draw up a form of government for them.

John Locke drew up a plan of government which they thought very fine, but which everybody now thinks was very foolish and absurd. I fancy he knew more about philosophy than he did about government. He called it the "Grand Model," and the noble lords thought they had a wonderful government indeed. There were to be earls and barons and lords, the same as in Europe. No one could vote who did not hold fifty acres. The poorer people were to be like so many slaves. They could not even leave one plantation for another without asking leave from the lord or baron who owned it.

What do you think the people did? You must not imagine they came across the ocean to be made slaves of. No, indeed! They cared no more for the "Grand Model" than if it was a piece of tissue paper. They settled where they pleased, and would not work for the earls and barons, and fought with the governors, and refused to pay the heavy taxes which the eight noble owners asked.

In time these noblemen got so sick of the whole business that they gave their province back to the king. It was then divided into two colonies, known as North Carolina and South Carolina. As for the lords and barons, nobody heard of them any more.

The people of the Carolinas had other things beside the Grand Model government to trouble them. There were savage Indians back in the country who attacked them and killed many of them. And there were pirates along the coast who attacked ships and killed all on board. But rice and indigo were planted, and afterwards cotton, and much tar and turpentine were got from the pine trees in North Carolina, and as the years went on, these colonies became rich and prosperous, and the people began to have a happy time.

Chapter 9

Georgia

I hope none of my young readers are tired of reading about kings and colonies. I am sure they must have enjoyed reading about John Smith and Miles Standish and William Penn and the rest of the great leaders. At any rate, there is only one more colony to talk about, and then we will be through with this part of the story. This is the colony of Georgia, which lies in the tract of land between South Carolina and Florida.

I am sure that when you are done reading this book you will be glad that you did not live two or three hundred years ago. Today every one can think as he pleases and do as he pleases, too, if he does not break the laws. And the laws are much more just and less cruel than they were in former times. Why, in those days, every man who owed money and could not pay it might be put in prison and kept there for years. He could not work there and earn money to pay his debts, and if his friends did not pay them, he might stay there till he died. As I have told you, even the good William Penn was put in prison for debt and kept there till his friends paid the money.

There were as many poor debtors in prison as there were thieves and villains. Some of them took sick and died, and some were starved to death by cruel jailers who would not give them anything to eat if they had no money to pay for food. One great and good man, named General James Oglethorpe, visited the prisons and was so sorry for the poor debtors he saw there that he asked the king to give him a piece of land in America where he could take some of these suffering people.

There was now not much land left to give. Settlements had been made all along the coast except south of the Carolinas, and the king told General Oglethorpe that he could have the land which lay there and could take as many debtors out of prison as he chose. He thought it would be a good thing to take them somewhere where they could work and earn their living. The king who was then on the throne was named King George, so Oglethorpe called his new colony Georgia.

It was now the year 1733, a hundred years after Lord Baltimore had come to Maryland. General Oglethorpe took many of the debtors out of prison, and very glad they were to get out, you may be sure. He landed with them on the banks of a fine river away down South, where he laid out a town which he named Savannah.

The happy debtors now found themselves in a broad and beautiful land, where they could prove whether they were ready to work or not. They were not long in doing this. Right away they began to cut down trees and build houses and plant fields, and very soon a pretty town was to be seen and food plants were growing in the fields. And very happy men and women these poor people were.

General Oglethorpe knew as well as William Penn that the land did not belong to the king. He sent for the Indian chiefs and told them the land was theirs and offered to pay them for it. They were quite willing to sell, and soon he had all the land he wanted, and what is more, he had the Indians for friends.

But if he had no trouble with the Indians, he had a good deal with the Spaniards of Florida. They said that Georgia was a part of Florida and that the English had no right there. And they sent an army and tried to drive them out.

I fancy they did not know that Oglethorpe was an old soldier, but he soon showed them that he knew how to fight. He drove back their armies and took their ships, and they quickly made up their minds that they had better let the English alone. There was plenty of land for both, for the Spaniards had only one town in Florida. This was St. Augustine.

Before long some Germans came from Europe and settled in the new colony. People came also from other parts of Europe. Corn was planted for food, and some colonists raised silkworms and made silk. But in the end, cotton came to be the chief crop of the colony.

General Oglethorpe lived to be a very old man. He did not die till long after the American Revolution. Georgia was then a flourishing state, and the little town he had started on the banks of the Savannah River was a fine city with broad streets, fine mansions, and beautiful shade trees. I think the poor old man must have been very proud of this charming city and of the great state which owed its start to him.

Chapter 10

The Native Americans

Now that you have been told about the settlement of the colonies, it is well to recall how many of them there were. Let us see. There were the Pilgrim and Puritan settlements of New England, Roger Williams's settlement in Rhode Island, the Dutch settlement in New York, the Quaker one in Pennsylvania, the Catholic settlement in Maryland, the Cavalier ones in Virginia and the Carolinas, and the Debtor settlement in Georgia. Then there were some smaller ones, making about a dozen in all. = 12

These stretched all along the coast, from Canada, the French country in the north, to Florida, the Spanish country in the south. The British were a long time in settling these places, for nearly 250 years passed after the time of Columbus before General Oglethorpe came to Georgia.

While all this was going on, what was becoming of the native people of the country, the Indians? I am afraid they were having a very hard time of it. The Spaniards made slaves of them and forced them to work so terribly hard in the mines and the fields that they died by the thousands. The French and the English fought with them and drove them away from their old homes, killing many of them.

And this has gone on and on ever since, until the Native Americans, who once spread over all this country, are now kept in a very small part of it.

What do you know about these Indians? I have been busy so far talking about the white men and what they did and have had no chance to tell you about the people they found on this continent and how they treated them. I think I must make this chapter an Indian one.

Well, then, when the Spanish came to the south, and the French came to the north, and the Dutch and the Swedes and the British to the middle country, they found everywhere a kind of people they had never seen before. Their skin was not white, like that of the people of Europe, nor black like that of the Africans, but of a reddish color, like that of copper. They had black eyes and hair, and high cheek-bones; they were tall and strong, and many of them very proud and dignified.

These people lived in a very wild fashion. They spent much of their time in hunting, fishing, and fighting. They raised some Indian corn and beans and were fond of tobacco, but most of their food was got from wild animals killed in the woods. They were as fond of fighting as they were of hunting. They were divided into tribes, some of which were nearly always at war with other tribes. They had no weapons but stone hatchets and bows and arrows, but they were able with these to kill many of their enemies. People say that they were badly treated by the whites, but they treated one another worse than the whites ever did.

The Indians were very cruel. The warriors shaved off all their hair except one lock, which was called the scalp lock. When one of them was killed in battle, this lock was used to pull off his scalp, or the skin of his head. They were very proud of these scalps, for they showed how many men they had killed.

When they took a prisoner, they would tie him to a tree and build a fire round him and burn him to death. And while he was burning, they would torture him all they could. We cannot feel so much pity for the Indians when we think of all this. No doubt the white men have treated them very unjustly, but they have stopped all these terrible cruelties, and that is something to be thankful for.

At the time I am speaking of, forests covered much of this great continent. They spread everywhere, and the Indians lived under their shade and had wonderful skill in following animals or enemies through their shady depths. They read the ground much as we read the pages of a book. A broken twig, a bit of torn moss, a footprint which we could not see, were full of meaning to them, and they would follow a trail for miles through the woods where we would not have been able to follow it a yard. Their eyes were trained to this kind of work, but in time some of the white men became as expert as the Indians and could follow a trail as well.

The Indians lived mostly in little huts covered with skins or bark, which they called wigwams. Some of the tribes lived in villages where there were large bark houses. But they did not stay much in their houses, for they liked better to be in the open air. Now they were hunting deer in the woods, now fishing or paddling their bark canoes in the streams, now smoking their pipes in front of their huts, now dancing their war dances or getting ready to fight.

The men did no work but hunting and fighting. The women had to do all other work, such as cooking, planting and gathering corn, building wigwams, and the like. They did some weaving of cloth, but most of their clothes were made of the skins of wild animals.

The warriors tried to make themselves as ugly as they could in war times, painting their faces in a horrid fashion and sticking feathers in their hair. They seemed to think they could scare their enemies by ugly faces.

I have spoken of the tribes of the Indians. Some of these tribes were quite large and were made up of a large number of men and women who lived together and spoke the same language. Each tribe was divided up into clans, or small family-like groups, and each clan had its sachem, or peace-chief. There were war-chiefs, also, who led them to battle. The sachems and chiefs governed the tribes and made such laws as they had.

Every clan had some animal which it called its totem, such as the wolf, bear, or fox. They were proud of their totems, and the form of the animal was tattooed on their breast. All the Indians were fond of dancing, and their war dances were as fierce and wild as they could make them.

The tribes in the south were not as savage as those in the north. They did more farming and had large and well-built villages. Some of them had temples and priests and looked upon the sun as a god. They kept a fire always burning in the temple, and seemed to think this fire was a part of their sun-god. They had a great chief who ruled over the tribe, and also a head war-chief, a high priest, and other rulers.

In the far west there were Indians who built houses that were almost like towns, for they had hundreds of rooms. A whole tribe could live in one of these great houses, sometimes as many as three thousand people. Other tribes lived in holes in the sides of steep rocks, where their enemies could not easily get at them. These are called Cliff-dwellers. And there were some who lived on top of high, steep hills, which were very hard to climb. These Indians raised large crops of corn and other plants.

Do you think, if you had been an Indian, you would have liked to see white people coming in ships across the waters and settling down in your country as if they owned it? They did not all pay for the land they took, like William Penn and General Oglethorpe. The most of them acted as if the country belonged to them, and it is no wonder the old owners of the country did not like it, or that there was fierce fighting between the white men and the Indians.

Do you remember the story of Canonicus and the snake skin, and that of Miles Standish and the chiefs? There was not much fighting then, but there was some soon after in Connecticut, whither a number of settlers had come from Boston and others from England. Here there was a warlike tribe called the Pequots, who became very angry on seeing the white men in their country.

They began to kill the whites whenever they found them

alone. Then the whites began to kill the Indians. Soon there was a deadly war. The Pequots had made a fort of trunks of trees, set close together in the ground. They thought they were safe in this form, but the English made an attack on it, got into it, and set fire to the Indian wigwams inside. The fight went on terribly in the smoke and flame until nearly all the Pequots were killed. Only two white men lost their lives. This so scared the Indians that it was forty years before there was another Indian war in New England.

I have told you about the good chief Massasoit, who was so kind to Roger Williams. He was a friend to the white men as long as he lived, but after his death his son Philip became one of their greatest enemies.

Philip's brother took sick and died after he had been to Plymouth, and the Indians thought that the people there had given him poison. Philip said that they would try to kill him next, and he made up his mind to fight them and drive them out of the country. The Indians had guns now and knew how to use them, and they began to shoot the white people as they went quietly along the roads.

Next they began to attack the villages of the whites. They would creep up at night, set the houses on fire, and shoot the men as they came out. The war went on for a long time in this way, and there were many terrible fights.

At one place the people, when they saw the Indians coming, all ran to a strong building called a block-house. The Indians came whooping and yelling around this and tried to set it on fire by shooting arrows with blazing rags on their points. Once the roof caught fire, but some of the men ran up and threw water on the flames.

Then the Indians got a cart and filled it with hay. Setting this on fire, they pushed it up against the house. It looked as if all the white men and women and children would be burned alive. The house caught fire and began to blaze. But just then came a shower of rain that put out the fire, and the people inside were saved once more. Before the Indians could do anything further, some white soldiers came and the Indians all ran into the woods.

There were other wonderful escapes, but many of the settlers were killed, and Philip began to think he would be able to drive them out of the country, as he wished to do. He was called King Philip, though he had no crown except a string of wampum—or bits of bored shell strung together and twined round his head—and no palace better than a bark hut, while his finest dress was a red blanket. It took very little to make an Indian king. The white men knew more about war than the Indians, and in the end they began to drive them back. One of their forts was taken, and the wigwams in it were set on fire, like those of the Pequots. A great many of the poor Indians perished in the flames.

The best fighter among the white men was Captain Church. He followed King Philip and his men to one hiding place after another, killing some and taking others prisoners. Among the prisoners were the wife and little son of the Indian king.

"It breaks my heart," said Philip, when he heard of this. "Now I am ready to die."

He did not live much longer. Captain Church chased him from place to place, till he came to Mount Hope, in Rhode Island, where Massasoit lived when Roger Williams came to him through the woods. Here King Philip was shot, and the war ended. It had lasted more than a year, and a large number had been killed on both sides. It is known in history as King Philip's War.

There were wars with the Indians in many other parts of the country. In Virginia the Indians made a plot to kill all the white people. They pretended to be very friendly and brought them meat and fish to sell. While they were talking quietly, the Indians drew their tomahawks and began to kill the whites. In that one morning, nearly three hundred and fifty were killed—men, women, and little children.

Hardly any of the settlers were left alive, except those in Jamestown, who were warned in time. They now attacked the

Indians, shooting down all they could find and killing a great many of them.

This was after the death of Powhatan, who had been a friend to the whites. About twenty years later, in 1644, another Indian massacre took place. After this, the Indians were driven far back into the country and did not give anymore trouble for thirty years. The last war with them broke out in 1675.

The Dutch in New York also had their troubles with the Indians. They paid for all the lands they took, but one of their governors was foolish enough to start a war that went on for two years. A worse trouble was that in North Carolina, where there was a powerful tribe called the Tuscaroras. These attacked the settlers and murdered numbers of them. But in the end they were driven out of the country.

The only colonies in which the Indians kept friendly for a long time were Pennsylvania and Georgia. We know the reason of this. William Penn and General Oglethorpe were wise enough to make friends with them at the start and continued to treat them with justice and friendliness, so that the Indians came to love these good men.

Indian Names

Lydia Huntley Sigourney

Ye say they all have passed away,
   That noble race and brave,
That their light canoes have vanished
From off the crested wave;
That, mid the forests where they roamed,
There rings no hunters' shout;
But their name is on your waters,
Ye may not wash it out.

'Tis where Ontario's billow
Like ocean's surge is curled,
Where strong Niagara's thunders wake
The echo of the world,
Where red Missouri bringeth
Rich tribute from the west,
And Rappahannock sweetly sleeps
On green Virginia's breast.

Ye say their cone-like cabins,
That clustered o'er the vale,
Have disappeared, as withered leaves
Before the autumn's gale;
But their memory liveth on your hills,
Their baptism on your shore,

Your everlasting rivers speak
Their dialect of yore.

Old Massachusetts wears it
Within her lordly crown,
And broad Ohio bears it
Amid his young renown.
Connecticut hath wreathed it
Where her quiet foliage waves,
And bold Kentucky breathes it hoarse
Through all her ancient caves.

Wachusett hides its lingering voice
Within its rocky heart,
And Alleghany graves its tone
Throughout his lofty chart.
Monadnock, on his forehead hoar,
Doth seal the sacred trust,
Your mountains built their monument,
Though ye destroy their dust.

Chapter 11
Royal Governors and Loyal Captains

D o any of my young readers know what is meant by a Charter? "Yes," I hear some of you say. "No," say others. Well, I must speak to the "No" party; the party that doesn't know and wants to know.

A charter is a written or printed document which grants certain rights or privileges to the party to whom it is given. It may come from a King or a Congress, or from any person in power, and be given to any other person who wishes the right to hold a certain property or to do some special thing.

Do you understand any better now? I am sorry I can not put it in plainer words. I think the best way will be to tell you about some charters which belong to American history. You should know that all the people who crossed the ocean to make new settlements on the Atlantic Coast had charters from the king of England. This was the case with the Pilgrims and the Puritans, with Roger Williams, William Penn, Lord Baltimore, and the others I have spoken about.

These charters were great documents written on parchment, and giving these people the right to settle on and own certain lands, to form certain kinds of government, and to do a variety of things which in England no one could do but the king and the parliament.

The colonies in New England were given the right to choose their own governors and make their own laws, and nobody, not even the king, could stop them from doing this. The king had given them this right, and no other king could take it away while they kept their charters.

Would you care to be told what took place afterwards? All kings, you should know, are not alike. Some are very mild and easy, and some are very harsh and severe. Some are willing for the people to have liberty, and some are not. The kings who gave the charters to New England were of the easy kind. But they were followed by kings of the hard kind, who thought that these people beyond the sea had too much liberty, and who wished to take away some of it.

Charles II, who gave some of these charters, was one of the easy kings and did not trouble himself about the people in the colonies. James II, who came after him, was one of the hard kings. He was a good deal of a tyrant and wanted to make the laws himself and take the right to do this from the people. After trying to rob the people of England of their liberties, he thought he would do the same thing with the people of America. "Those folks across the seas are having too good a time," he thought. "They have too many rights and privileges, and I must take some of them away. I will let them know that I am their master."

But they had their charters, which gave them these rights; so the wicked king thought the first thing for him to do was to take their charters away from them. Then their rights would be gone, and he could make for them a new set of laws and force them to do everything he wished.

What King James did was to send a nobleman named Sir Edmund Andros to New England to rule as royal governor. He was the agent of the king and was to do all that the king ordered. One of the first things he was to do was to rob the people of their charters. You see, even a tyrant king did not like to go against the charters, for a charter was a sacred pledge.

Well, the new governor went about ordering the people to give him their charters. One of the places he went to was Hartford,

Connecticut, and there he told the officers of the colony that they must deliver up their charter; the king had said so, and the king's word must be obeyed.

If any of you had lived in Connecticut in those days I know how you would have felt. The charter gave the people a great deal of liberty, and they did not wish to part with it. I know that you and I would have felt the same way. But what could they do? If they did not give it up peacefully Governor Andros might come again with soldiers and take it from them by force. So the governor and the lawmakers and officials were in a great fret about what they should do.

They asked Governor Andros to come to the statehouse and talk over the matter. Some of them fancied they could get him to leave them their charter, though they might have known better. There they sat—the governor in the lofty chair of state, the others seated in a half circle before him. There was a broad table between them, and on this lay the great parchment of the charter. Some of those present did a great deal of talking. They said how good King Charles had given them the charter, and how happy they had been under it, and how loyal they were to good King James, and they begged Governor Andros not to take it from them. But they might as well have talked to the walls. He had his orders from the king and was one of the men who do just what they are told.

While the talk was going on, a strange thing happened. It was night, and the room was lit up with a few tallow candles. Of course you know that these were the best lights people had at that time; electric lights had never been heard of. And it was before the time of matches. The only way to make a light in those days was by use of the flint and steel, which was a very slow method indeed.

Suddenly, while one of the Hartford men was talking and the governor was looking at him in a tired sort of way, all the lights in the room went out, and the room was in deep darkness. Everybody jumped up from their chairs and there was no end of bustle and confusion, and likely enough some pretty hard words were said.

They had to hunt in the dark for the flint and steel; and then there came snapping of steel on flint, and falling of sparks on tinder, so that it was some time before the candles were lit again.

When this was done, the governor opened his eyes very wide, for the table was empty; the charter was gone. Everybody looked for it, right and left, in and out, in drawers and closets, but it was nowhere to be found. Very likely the most of them did not want to find it. At any rate, the governor had to go away without the charter, and years passed before anybody saw it again.

Do you not wish to know what became of it? We are told that it had been taken by a bold young soldier named Captain Wadsworth. While all the people in the room were looking at the one who was making his speech, the Captain quickly took off his cloak and gave it a quick fling over the candles, so that in a moment they were all put out. Then he snatched up the charter from the table and slipped quietly out of the room. While they were busy snapping the flint and steel, he was hurrying down the street towards a great oak tree which was more than a hundred years old. This tree was hollow in its heart, and there was a hole in its side which opened into the hollow. Into this hole Captain Wadsworth pushed the charter, and it fell into the hollow space. I do not think any of us would have thought of looking there for it. I know nobody did at that time, and there it lay for years, until the tyrant King James was driven from the throne and a new king had taken his place. Then it was joyfully brought out, and the people were ever so glad to see it again.

The old tree stood for many years in the main street of the town, and became famous as the Charter Oak. The people loved and were proud of it as long as it stood.

Do you not think that Captain Wadsworth was a bold and daring man, and one who knew just what to do in times of trouble? If you do not, I fancy you will when I have told you another story about him.

This took place after the charter had been taken from the

oak and brought to the state-house again. At this time there was a governor in New York named Fletcher, who claimed that the king had given him the right to command the militia, or citizen soldiers, of Connecticut. So he came to Hartford, where Captain Wadsworth was in command, and where the people did not want any stranger to have power over them. He told the captain what he had come for and that he had a commission to read to the soldiers.

The militia were called out and drawn up in line in the public square of the town, and Governor Fletcher came before them, full of his importance. He took out of his pocket the paper which he said gave him the right to command and began to read it in a very proud and haughty manner. But he had not read ten words when Captain Wadsworth told the drummers to beat their drums, and before you could draw your breath, there was such a rattle and roll of noise that not a word could be heard.

"Silence!" cried Fletcher. "Stop those drums!" The drums stopped, and he began to read again.

"Drum!" ordered Wadsworth in a loud tone, and such a noise began that a giant's voice would have been drowned.

"Silence!" again shouted Fletcher. He was very red in the face by this time.

"Drum, I say!" roared the captain.

Then he turned to the governor and said, laying his hand on his sword, "I command these men, Governor Fletcher, and if you interrupt me again I will make the sun shine through you in a minute." And he looked as if he meant what he said. All the governor's pomp and consequence were gone, and his face turned from red to pale. He hastily thrust the paper back into his pocket and was not long in leaving Hartford for New York. No doubt he thought that Connecticut was not a good place for royal governors.

Suppose I now tell you the story of another royal governor and another bold captain. This was down in Virginia, but it was long after Captain Smith was dead and after Virginia had become a large and prosperous colony.

The king sent there a governor named Berkeley, who acted as if he was master and all the people were his slaves. They did not like to be treated this way; but Berkeley had soldiers under his command, and they were forced to obey. While this was going on, Indians began to murder the settlers. The governor ought to have stopped them, but he was afraid to call out the people, and he let the murders go on.

There was a young man named Nathaniel Bacon who asked Governor Berkeley to let him raise some men to fight the Indians. The governor refused. But this did not stop brave young Bacon, for he called out a force of men and drove off the murdering Indians.

Governor Berkeley was very angry at this. He said that Bacon was a traitor and ought to be treated like one, and that the men with him were rebels. Bacon at once marched with his men against Jamestown, and the haughty governor ran away as fast as he could.

But while Bacon and his men were fighting the Indians again, Governor Berkeley came back and talked more than ever about rebels and traitors. This made Bacon and the people with him very angry. To be treated in this way while they were saving the people from the Indian knife and tomahawk was too bad. They marched against Jamestown again. This time the governor did not run away, but prepared to defend the place with soldiers and cannon.

But they did not fire their guns. Bacon had captured some of the wives of the principal men, and he put them in front of his line as he advanced. The governor did not dare bid his soldiers to fire on these women, so he left the town again in a hurry.

Bacon made up his mind that Governor Berkeley should not come back to Jamestown again. He had the town set on fire and burned to the ground. Some of the men with him set fire to their own houses, so that they should not give shelter to the governor and his men. That was the end of Jamestown. It was never rebuilt. Only ashes remained of the first English town in America.

We cannot tell what might have happened if brave young

Bacon had lived. As it was, he took sick and died. His men now had no leader and soon dispersed. Then the governor came back full of fury and began to hang all those who opposed him. He might have put a great many of them to death if the king had not stopped him and ordered him back to England. This was King Charles II, whose father had been put to death by Cromwell. He was angry at what Governor Berkeley had done, and said:

"That old fool has hung more men in that naked land than I did for the murder of my father."

Chapter 12
Old Times in the Colonies

What a wonderful change has come over this great country of ours since the days of our forefathers! Look at our great cities, with their grand buildings and their miles of streets, with swift-speeding cars and great stores lit by electric lights, and huge factories filled with marvelous machines! And look at our broad fields filled with cattle or covered by growing crops and divided by splendid highways and railroads thousands of miles in length! Is it not all very wonderful?

"But has it not always been this way?" some very young persons ask. "I have lived so many years and have never seen anything else."

My dear young friend, if you had lived fifty or sixty years, as many of us older folks have, you would have seen very different things. And if we had lived as long ago as our great-great-grandfathers did, and then come back again today, I fancy our eyes would open wider than Governor Andros's did when he saw that the charter was gone.

In those days, as I told you, when any one wanted to make a light, he could not strike a match or flip a switch as we do, but must hammer away with flint and steel, and then had nothing better than a homemade tallow candle to light. Why, I am sure that many of you never even saw a pair of snuffers, which people then used to cut off the candle wick.

Some of you who live in old houses with dusty lofts under the roof, full of old furniture, have, no doubt, found there odd-looking wooden frames and wheels, and queer old tools of various kinds. Sometimes these wheels are brought downstairs and set in the hall as something to be proud of. And the old eight-day clocks stand here, too, with their loud "tick-tock," buzzing and ticking away today as if they had not done so for a hundred years.

The wheels I speak of are the old spinning wheels, with which our great-great-grandmothers spun flax into thread. This thread they wove into homespun cloth on old-fashioned looms. All work of this kind used to be done at home, though now it is done in great factories, and we buy our clothes in the stores instead of spinning and weaving and sewing them in the great old kitchens before the wood-fire on the hearth.

Really, I am afraid many of you do not know how people lived in the old times. They are often spoken of as the "good old times." I fancy you will hardly think so when I have told you something more about them. Would you think it very good to have to get up in a freezing cold room, and go down and pump ice-cold water to wash your face, and go out in the snow to get wood to make the fire, and shiver for an hour before the house began to warm up? That is only one of the things you would not think good. I shall certainly have to stop here and tell you about how people lived in old times, and then you can say if you would like to go back to them.

Would any boy and girl among you care to live in a little one-story house, made of rough logs laid one on another, and wish a roof of thatch—that is, of straw or reeds, or anything that would keep out the rain? Houses, I mean, with only one or two rooms, and some of them with chimneys made of wood, plastered with clay on the inside so that they could not be set on fire. These were the oldest houses. Later on people began to build larger houses, many of which were made of brick or stone. But I am afraid there was not much comfort in the best of them. They had no stoves, and were heated by great stone fireplaces, where big logs of wood were burned. They made a bright and cheerful blaze, it is true, but most of the heat went roaring up the wide chimney, and only a little of it got out into the room. In the winter the people lived in their kitchens, with the blazing wood-fire for heat and light, and at bedtime went shivering off to ice-cold rooms. Do you think you would have enjoyed that?

They had very little furniture, and the most of what they had was rude and rough, much of it chopped out of the trees by the farmer's axe. Some of the houses had glass windows—little diamond-shaped panes, set in lead frames—but most of them had nothing but oiled paper, which kept out as much light as it let in.

All the cooking was done on the great kitchen hearth, where the pots were hung on iron cranes and the pans set on the blazing coals. They did not have as much food to cook as we have. Mush and milk, or pork and beans, were their usual food, and their bread was mostly made of rye or cornmeal. The boys and girls who had nice books they wanted to read often had to do so by the light of the kitchen fire; but I can tell you that books were very scarce things in those days.

If any of us had lived then I know how glad we would have been to see the bright spring time, with its flowers and warm sunshine. But we might have shivered again when we thought of next winter.

Of course, the people had some good times. They had Thanksgiving day, when the table was filled with good things to eat, and election-day and training-day, when they had outdoor sports. And they had quilting- and husking-parties, and spinning-bees, and sleigh-rides and picnics and other amusements. A wedding was a happy time, and even a funeral was followed by a great dinner. But after all, there was much more hard work than holiday, and nearly everybody had to labor long and got little for it. They were making themselves homes and a country, you know, and it was a very severe task. We, today, are getting the good of their work.

Down South people had more comfort. The weather was not nearly so cold, so they did not have to keep up such blazing fires or shiver in their cold beds. Many of the rich planters built themselves large mansions of wood or brick, and brought costly furniture from England, and lived in great show with gold and silverware on their sideboards and fine coaches drawn by handsome horses when they went abroad.

In New York the Dutch built quaint old houses, of the kind used in Holland. In Philadelphia the Quakers lived in neat two-storied houses with wide orchards and gardens round them, where they raised plenty of fruit. When any one opened a shop, he would hang out a basket, a wooden anchor, or some such sign to show what kind of goods he had to sell.

In New England Sunday was kept in a very strict fashion, for the people were very religious. It was thought wicked to play, or even to laugh, on Sunday, and everybody had to go to church. All who did not go were punished. And, mercy on us, what sermons they preached in those cold old churches, prosing away sometimes for three or four hours at a time! The boys and girls had to listen to them, as well as the men and women. If they got sleepy and went off into a snooze, they were soon wide awake again. For the constable went up and down the aisles with a long staff in his hand. This had a rabbit's foot on one end of it and a rabbit's tail on the other. If he saw one of the women asleep, he would draw the rabbit's tail over her face. But if a boy took a nap, down would come the rabbit's foot in a sharp rap on his head, and up he would start very wide awake.

Do you think those were "good old times"? I imagine some of you will fancy they were "bad old times." But they were not nearly so bad as you may think. For you must bear in mind that the people knew nothing of many of the things we enjoy. They were used to hard work and plain food and coarse furniture and rough clothes and cold rooms, and were more hardy and could stand more than people who sleep in furnace-heated rooms and have their tables heaped with all kinds of fruits and vegetables and meats.

But there was one thing that could not have been pleasant, and that was their being afraid all the time of Indians, and having to carry muskets with them even when they went to church. All around them were the forests in which the Indians roamed, and their cruel yell might be heard at any time, or a sharp arrow whiz out from the thick leaves.

The farm-houses were built like forts, and in all the villages were strong buildings called block-houses to which everybody could run in times of danger. In these the second story spread out over the first and there were holes in the floor through which the men could fire down on the Indians below. But it makes us tremble to think that, at any time, the traveler or farmer might be shot down by a lurking Indian, or might be seized and burned alive. We can hardly wonder that the people grew to hate the Indians and to kill them or drive them away.

There was much game in the woods and the rivers were full of fish, so that many of the people spent their time in hunting and fishing. They got to be as expert in this as the Indians themselves, and some of them could follow a trail as well as the most sharp-sighted Indian.

Chapter 13

Daniel Boone

Some of you may have read Fenimore Cooper's novels of Indian life and know what a wonderful hunter and Indian trailer old Natty Bumppo was. But we do not need to go to novels to read about great hunters, for the life of Daniel Boone is as full of adventure as that of any of the heroes of Indian life.

Daniel Boone was the most famous hunter this country has ever known. The country he lived in was as wild as that found by the first settlers of the country. When he was only a little boy, he went into the deep woods and lived there by himself for several days, shooting game and making a fire to cook it by. He made himself a little hut of boughs and sods, and lived there like an Indian, and there is where his father and friends found him when they came seeking him in the woods.

Years afterwards he crossed the high mountains of North Carolina and went into the great forest of Kentucky, where only Indians and wild animals lived. For a long time he stayed there by himself, with the Indians hunting and trying to kill him. But he was too wide awake for the smartest of them all.

One time, when they were close on his trail, he got away from them by catching hold of a loose grapevine and making a long swinging jump, and then running on. When the Indians got there, they lost the marks of his footprints and gave up the chase. At another time when he was taken prisoner, he got up, took one of their guns, and slipped away from them without one of them waking up.

Many years afterwards, when he and others had built a fort in Kentucky, and brought out their wives and children, Boone's daughters and two other girls were carried off by Indians while they were out picking wild flowers.

Boone and other hunters were soon on their trail, and followed it by the broken bushes and bits of torn dress which the wide-awake little girls had left behind them. In this way they came up to the Indians while they were eating their supper, fired on them, and then ran up and rescued the girls. These young folks did not go out of the fort to pick wild flowers after that.

Once Daniel Boone was taken prisoner, and would have been burned alive if an old woman had not taken him for her son. The Indians painted his face and made him dress like an Indian and live with them as one of themselves. But one day he heard them talking, and found out that they were going to attack the fort where all his friends were. Then he slipped out of the village and ran away. He had a long journey to make, and the Indians followed him close. But he walked in the water to hide his footsteps, and lived on roots and berries, for fear they would hear his gun if he shot any game. In the end he got back safe to the fort. He found it in bad condition, but he set the men to make it strong, and when the Indians came they were beaten off.

Daniel Boone lived to be a very old man, and kept going farther west to get away from the new people who were coming into the Kentucky forest. He said he wanted "elbow room." He spent all the rest of his life hunting, and the Indians looked on him as the greatest woodsman and the most wonderful hunter the white men ever had.

Chapter 14
A Hero of the Colonies

D o you not think there are a good many interesting stories
in American history? I have told you some and I could
tell you many more. I am going to tell you one now, about a
brave young man who had a great deal to do with the making
of our glorious country. But to reach it we will have to take a
step backward more than two hundred years. That is a pretty long
step, isn't it? It takes us away back to about the year 1750. But
people had been coming into this country for more than a hundred
and fifty years before that, and there were a great many men and
women in America at that time.

These people came from Spain and France and Great Britain
and Holland and Germany and Sweden and other countries
besides. The Spaniards had spread through many regions in the
south; the French had gone west by way of the Great Lakes and
then down the Mississippi River; but the British were settled close
to the ocean, and the country back of them was still forest land,
where only Indians and wild beasts lived. That is the way things
were situated at the time of the story which I now propose to tell.

The young man I am about to speak of knew almost as much
about life in the deep woods as Daniel Boone, the great hunter,
of whom I have just told you. Why, when he was only sixteen
years old, he and another boy went far back into the wild country

of Virginia to survey, or measure, the lands there for a rich land-holder.

The two boys crossed the rough mountains and went into the broad valley of the Shenandoah River, and for months they lived there alone in the broad forest. There were no roads through the woods and they had to make their own paths. When they were hungry, they would shoot a wild turkey or a squirrel or sometimes a deer. They would cook their meat by holding it on a stick over a fire of fallen twigs, and for plates they would cut large chips from a tree with their axe.

All day long they worked in the woods, measuring the land with a long chain. At night they would roll themselves in their blankets and go to sleep under the trees. If the weather was cold they gathered wood and made a fire. Very likely they enjoyed it all, for boys are fond of adventure. Sometimes a party of Indians would come up and be very curious to know what these white boys were doing. But the Indians were peaceful then and did not try to harm them. One party amused the young surveyors by dancing a war dance before them. A fine time they had in the woods, where they stayed alone for months. When they came back, the land-holder was much pleased with their work.

Now let us go on for five years, when the backwoods boy-surveyor had become a young man twenty-one years of age. If we could take ourselves back to the year 1753 and plunge into the woods of western Pennsylvania, we might see this young man again in the deep forest, walking along with his rifle in hand and his pack on his back. He had with him an old frontiersman named Gill and an Indian who acted as their guide through the forest.

The Indian was a treacherous fellow. One day, when they were not looking, he fired his gun at them from behind a tree. He did not hit either of them. Some men would have shot him, but they did not; they let him go away and walked on alone through the deep woods. They built a fire that night, but they did not sleep before it, for they were afraid the Indian might come back and try to kill them while they were sleeping. So they left it burning and walked on a few miles and went to sleep without a fire.

A few days after that they came to the banks of a wide river. You may find it on your map of Pennsylvania. It is called the Alleghany River, and runs into the Ohio. It had been frozen, for it was winter time; but now the ice was broken and floating swiftly down the stream.

What were they to do? They had to get across that stream. The only plan they could think of was to build a raft out of logs and try to push it through the ice with long poles. This they did, and were soon out on the wild river and among the floating ice.

It was a terrible passage. The great cakes of ice came swirling along and striking like heavy hammers against the raft, almost hard enough to knock it to pieces. One of these heavy ice cakes struck the pole of the young traveller, and gave him such a shock that he fell from the raft into the freezing cold water. He had a hard enough scramble to get back on the raft again.

After a while they reached a little island in the stream and got ashore. There was no wood on it and they could not make a fire, so they had to walk about all night to keep from freezing. The young man was wet to the skin, but he had young blood and did not suffer as much as the older man with him. When morning came they found that the ice was frozen fast between the island and the other shore, so all they had to do was to walk across it.

These were not the only adventures they had, but they got safe back to Virginia, from which they had set out months before.

Do you want to know who this young traveller was? His name was George Washington. That is all I need to say. Any one who does not know who George Washington was is not much of an American. But quite likely you do not guess what he was doing in the woods so far away from his home. He had been sent there by the governor of Virginia, and I shall have to tell you why.

But first you must go back with me to an earlier time. The time I mean is when the French were settling in Canada along the

St. Lawrence River, and going west over the lakes, and floating in canoes down the Mississippi River to the Gulf of Mexico. Wherever they went they built forts and claimed the country for their king. At the same time the English were settling along the Atlantic shores and pushing slowly back into the country.

You should know that the French and the English were not the best of friends. They had their wars in Europe, and every time they got into war there, they began to fight in America also. This made terrible times in the new country. The French had many of the Indians on their side, and they marched through the woods and attacked some of the English towns, and the cruel Indians murdered many of the poor settlers who had done them no harm. There were three such wars, lasting for many years, and a great many innocent men, women, and children, who had nothing to do with the wars in Europe, lost their lives. This is what we call war. It is bad enough now, but it was worse still in those days.

The greatest of all the wars between the French and the English was still to come. Between the French forts on the Mississippi and the English settlements on the Atlantic there was a vast forest land, and both the French and the English said it belonged to them. In fact, it did not belong to either of them, but to the Indians; but the white men never troubled themselves about the rights of the old owners of the land.

While the English were talking, the French were acting. About 1750 they built two or three forts in the country south of Lake Erie. What they wanted was the Ohio River, with the rich and fertile lands which lay along that stream. Building those forts was the first step. The next step would be to send soldiers to the Ohio and build forts there also.

When the English heard what the French were doing, they became much alarmed. If they did not do something very quickly, they would lose all this great western country. The governor of Virginia wished to know what the French meant to do, and he thought the best way to find out was to ask them. So he picked out the young backwoods surveyor, George Washington, and sent him through the great forest to the French forts.

Washington was very young for so important a duty. But he was tall and strong and quick-witted, and he was not afraid of any man or anything. And he knew all about life in the woods. So he was chosen, and far west he went over plain and mountain, now on horseback and now on foot, following the Indian trails through the forest, until at last he came to the French forts.

The French officers told him that they had come there to stay. They were not going to give up their forts to please the governor of Virginia. And Washington's quick eyes saw that they were getting canoes ready to go down the streams to the Ohio River the next spring. This was the news the young messenger was taking back to the governor when he had his adventures with the Indian and the ice.

If any of you know anything about how wars are brought on, you may well think there was soon going to be war in America. Both parties wanted the land, and both were ready to fight to get it; and when people feel that way, fighting is not far off.

Indeed, the spring of 1754 was not far advanced before both sides were on the move. Washington had picked out a beautiful spot for a fort. This was where the two rivers which form the Ohio come together. On that spot the city of Pittsburg now stands; but then it was a very wild place.

As soon as the governor heard Washington's report, he sent a party of men in great haste to build a fort at that point. But in a short time, a larger party of French came down the Allegheny River in canoes and drove the English workmen away. Then they finished the fort for themselves and called it Fort Duquesne.

Meanwhile Washington was on his way back. A force of four hundred Virginians had been sent out under an officer named Colonel Frye. But the Colonel died on the march, and young Washington, then only twenty-two years old, found himself at the head of a regiment of soldiers and about to start a great war. Was it not a difficult position for so young a man? Not many men of that age would have known what to do, but George Washington was not an ordinary man.

While the Virginians were marching west, the French were marching south, and it was not long before they came together. A party of French hid in a thicket to watch the English, and Washington, thinking they were there for no good, ordered his men to fire. They did so, and the leader of the French was killed. This was the first shot in the coming war.

But the youthful commander soon found that the French were too strong for him. He built a sort of fort at a place called Great Meadows, and named it Fort Necessity. It was hardly finished before the French and Indians came swarming all around it and a severe fight began.

The Virginians fought well, but the French were too strong and fired into the fort till Washington had to surrender. This took place on July 4, 1754, just twenty-two years before the American Declaration of Independence. Washington and his men were allowed to march home with their arms, and the young colonel was very much praised when he got home, for everybody thought he had done his work in a very good way.

When the news of this battle crossed the ocean, there was great excitement in England and France, and both countries sent soldiers to America. Those from England were under a general named Braddock, a man who knew all about fighting in England, but knew nothing about fighting in America. And what was worse, he would let nobody tell him. Washington generously tried to do so, but he got pointedly snubbed by the proud British general for his pains.

After a while, away marched General Braddock with his British soldiers in their fine red coats. Washington went with him with a body of Virginians dressed in plain colony clothes. On and on they went, through the woods and over the mountains, cutting down trees and opening a road for their wagons, and bravely beating their drums and waving their flags. At length they came near Fort Duquesne, the drums still beating, the flags still flying, the gun barrels glittering in the bright sunshine.

"Let me go ahead with my Virginians," said Washington. "They know all about Indian fighting."

"That for your Indians!" said Braddock, snapping his fingers. "They will not stay in their hiding places long when my men come up."

Soon after, they came into a narrow place with steep banks and thick bushes all around. And suddenly loud Indian war-whoops and the crack of guns came from those bushes. Not a man could be seen, but bullets flew like hail-stones among the red-coats. The soldiers fired back, but they wasted their bullets on the bushes. Washington and his men ran into the woods and got behind trees like the Indians, but Braddock would not let his men do the same, and they were shot down like sheep. At length General Braddock fell wounded, and then his brave red-coats turned and ran for their lives. Very likely not a man of them would have got away if Washington and his men had not kept back the French and the Indians.

This defeat was a bad business for the poor settlers, for the Indians began murdering them on all sides, and during all the rest of the war Washington was kept busy fighting with these Indians. Not till four years afterward was he able to take Fort Duquesne from the French.

Chapter 15

The French and Indian War

Have any of my young readers read the beautiful poem of "Evangeline," written by the poet Longfellow? Very likely it is too old for you, though the time will come when you will read it and enjoy it very much. Evangeline was a pretty and pious woman who lived in a French settlement called Acadia, on the Atlantic coast. You will not find this name on any of your maps, but must look for Nova Scotia, by which name Acadia is now known. The story of Evangeline tells us about the cruel way in which the poor Acadians were treated by the English. It is a sad and pathetic story, as you will see when you have read it.

It was one of the wicked results of the war between the French and the English. There were many cruel deeds in this war, and the people who suffered the most were those who had the least to do with the fighting. In one place a quiet, happy family of father, mother, and children, living on a lonely farm and not dreaming of any danger, suddenly hear the wild war-whoop of the Indians and soon see their door broken open and their house blazing, and are carried off into cruel captivity—those who are not killed on the spot. In another place all the people of a village are driven from their comfortable homes by soldiers and forced to wander and beg their bread in distant lands. And all this takes place because the kings of England and France, three thousand miles away, are quarreling about some lands which do not belong to either of them. If those who brought on wars had to suffer for them, they would soon come to an end. But they revel and feast in their splendid palaces while poor and innocent people do the suffering. The war that began in the wilds of western Pennsylvania, between the French and Indians and the English, lasted seven years, from 1754 to 1761. During that time there were many terrible battles, and thousands of soldiers were killed, and there was much suffering and slaughter among the people, and burning of houses, and destruction of property, and horrors of all sorts.

It is called the French and Indian War because there were many Indians on the side of the French. There were some on the side of the English, also.

I must now ask you to look on a map of the state of New York, if you have one. There you will see that the Hudson River runs up north from the city of New York, past Albany, the capital of the state, and ends in a region of mountains. Near its upper waters is a long, narrow lake named Lake George, which is full of beautiful islands. North of that is a much larger lake named Lake Champlain, which reaches up nearly to Canada.

The British had forts on the Hudson River and Lake George and the French on Lake Champlain, and also between the two lakes, where stood the strong Fort Ticonderoga. It was around these forts and along these lakes that most of the fighting took place. For a long time the French had the best of it. The British lost many battles and were driven back. But they had the most soldiers, and in the end, they began to defeat the French and drive them back, and Canada became the seat of war. But let me tell you the story of the Acadians.

Acadia was a country which had been settled by the French a long, long time before, away back in 1604, before there was an English settlement in America. Captain John Smith, you know, came in 1607, three years afterwards. It was a very fertile country, and the settlers planted fields of grain and orchards of apples and other fruits, and lived a very happy life with neat houses and plenty of good food, and in time the whole country became a rich farming land.

But the British would not let these happy farmers alone. Every time there was trouble with the French, soldiers were sent to Acadia. It was captured by the British in 1690, but was given back to France in 1697, when that war ended. It was taken again by the British in the war that began in 1702, and this time it was not given back. Even its pretty name of Acadia was taken away, and it was called Nova Scotia, which is not nearly so pretty a name.

Thus it was that, when the new war with France began, Acadia was held as a province of Great Britain. To be sure the most of its people were descended from the old French settlers and did not like their British masters, but they could not help themselves and went on farming in their old fashion. They were ignorant, simple-minded countrymen, who looked upon France as their country and were not willing to be British subjects.

The British did not hold the whole of Acadia. The country now called New Brunswick, which lies north of Nova Scotia, was part of it and was still held by the French. In 1755 the British government decided to attempt the capture of this country and sent out soldiers for that purpose. Fighting began, but the French defended themselves bravely, and the British found they had a hard task to perform.

What made it worse for them was that some of the Acadians, who did not want to see the British succeed, acted as spies upon them and told the French soldiers about their movements, so that the French were everywhere ready for them. And the Acadians helped the French in other ways and gave the British a great deal of trouble.

This may have been wrong, but it was natural. Every one feels like helping his friends against his enemies. But you may be sure that it made the British very angry, and in the end they took a cruel resolution. This was to send all the Acadians away from their native land to far-off, foreign countries. It was not easy to tell who were acting as spies, so the English government ordered them all to be removed. They were told they might stay if they would swear to be true subjects of the king of England, but this the most of them would not do, for they were French at heart and looked on King Louis of France as their true and rightful ruler.

Was not this very cruel? There were hundreds of boys and girls like yourselves among these poor Acadians, who had happy homes and loved to work and play in their pretty gardens and green fields, and whose fathers and mothers did no harm to any one. But because a few busy men gave news to the French, all of these were to be torn from their comfortable homes and sent far away to wander in strange lands, where many of them would have to beg for bread. It was a heartless act, and the world has ever since said so, and among all the cruel things the British have done, the removal of the Acadians from their homes is looked upon as one of the worst.

When soldiers are sent to do a cruel thing, they are very apt to do it in the most brutal fashion. The Acadians did not know what was to be done. It was kept secret for fear they might run away and hide. A large number of soldiers were sent out, and they spread like a net over a wide stretch of country. Then they marched together and drove the people before them. The poor farmers might be at their dinners or working in their fields, but they were told that they must stop everything and leave their homes at once, for they were to be sent out of the country. Just think of it! What a grief and terror they must have been in!

They were hardly given time to gather the few things they could carry with them, and on all sides they were driven like so many sheep to the seaside town of Annapolis, to which ships had been brought to carry them away. More than six thousand of these unhappy people, old and young, men, women, and little ones, were gathered there; many of them weeping bitterly, many more with looks of despair on their faces, all of them sad at heart.

Around them were soldiers to keep them from running away.

They were made to get on the ships in such haste that families were often separated, husband and wife or children and their mothers being put on different ships and sent to different places. And for fear that some of them might come back again, their houses were burned and their farms laid waste. Many of them went to the French settlements in Louisiana, and others to other parts of America. Poor exiles! they were scattered widely over the earth. Some of them in time came back to their loved Acadia, but the most of them never saw it again. It was this dreadful act about which Longfellow wrote in his poem of Evangeline.

Now I must tell you how the French and Indian War ended. The French had two important cities in Canada: Montreal and Quebec. Quebec was built on a high and steep hill and was surrounded by strong walls, behind which were more than eight thousand soldiers. It was not an easy city to capture.

A large British fleet was sent against it, and also an army of eight thousand men under General Wolfe. For two of three months they fired at the city from the river below, but the French scorned them from their steep hill-top. At length, General Wolfe was told of a narrow path by which he might climb the hill. One dark night he tried it, and by daybreak a large body of men had reached the hill-top and had dragged up a number of cannon with them.

When the French saw this, they were frightened. They hurried out of the city, thinking they could drive the English over the precipice before any more of them got up. They were mistaken in this. The English met them boldly, and in the battle that followed they gained the victory, and Quebec fell into their hands.

General Wolfe was mortally wounded, but when he was told that the French were in flight, he said, "God be praised! I die happy."

Montcalm, the French general, also fell wounded. When he knew that he must die, he said, "So much the better; I shall not live to see the surrender of Quebec."

The next year Montreal was taken, and the war ended. And

in the treaty of peace, France gave up all her colonies in America. England got Canada and Spain got Louisiana. All North America now belonged to two nations: England and Spain.

Chapter 16
Causes of the Revolution

I should be glad to have some of you take a steamboat ride up the broad Hudson River, past the city of New York, and onward in the track of the "Half Moon," Henry Hudson's ship. If you did so, you would come in time to the point where this ship stopped and turned back. Here, where Hudson and his Dutch sailors saw only a great spread of forest trees, stretching far back from the river bank, our modern travelers would see the large and handsome city of Albany, the capital of the State of New York.

This is one of the hundreds of fine cities which have grown up in our country since Henry Hudson's time. Two hundred years ago it was a small place, not much larger than many of our villages. But even then it was of importance, for in it was taken the first step towards our great Union of States. I shall have to tell you what this step was, for you will certainly want to know.

Well, at the time I speak of there was no such thing as an American Union. There were thirteen colonies, reaching from New Hampshire down to Georgia. But each of these was like a little nation of its own; each had its own government, made its own laws, and fought its own fights. This was well enough in one way, but it was not so well in another. At one time the people had the Indians to fight with, at another time the French, and sometimes both of these together, and many of them thought that they could do their fighting better if they were united into one country.

So in the year 1754 the colonies sent some of their best men to Albany, to talk over this matter and see if a union of the colonies could not be made. This is what I meant when I said that the first step towards the American Union was taken at Albany.

Of these men, there is only one I shall say anything about. This man's name you should know and remember, for he was one of the noblest and wisest men that ever lived in this country. His name was Benjamin Franklin. Forty years before this time, he was a little Boston boy at work in his father's shop, helping him make candles. Afterwards he learned how to print, and then, in 1723, he went to Philadelphia, where he soon had a shop and a newspaper office, and in time became rich.

There was nothing going on that Franklin did not take part in. In his shop he bound books, he made ink, he sold rags, soap, and coffee. He was not ashamed of honest work, and would take off his coat and wheel his papers along the street in a wheelbarrow. He started many institutions in Philadelphia which are now very important. Among these there are a great university, a large hospital, and a fine library. No doubt you have read how he brought down the lightning from the clouds along the string of a kite, and proved that lightning is the same thing as electricity. And he took an active part in all the political movements of the time. That is why he came to be sent to Albany in 1754, as a member of the Albany Convention.

Franklin always did things in ways that set people to thinking. When he went to Albany he took with him copies of a queer picture which he had printed in his newspaper. This was a snake cut into thirteen pieces. Under each piece was the first letter of the name of a colony, such as "P" for Pennsylvania. Beneath the whole were the words "Unite or die."

That was like Franklin; he was always doing something odd. The cut-up snake stood for the thirteen divided colonies. What Franklin meant was that they could not exist alone. A snake is not of much account when it is chopped up into bits, but it is a dangerous creature when it is whole. He proposed that there should be a grand council of all the colonies, a sort of Congress, meeting every year in Philadelphia, which was the most central large city. Over them all was to be a governor-general appointed by the king. This council could make laws, lay taxes, and perform other important duties.

That is enough to say about Franklin's plan, for it was not accepted. It was passed by the convention, it is true, but the king would not have it and the colonies did not want it; so the snake still lay stretched out along the Atlantic in thirteen pieces. Then came the great war with the French of which I have told you. After that was over, things came to pass which in the end forced the colonies to combine. Thus Franklin's plan, or something like it, was in time carried out, but for many years the country was in a terrible state. This is what I am now going to tell you about.

You should know that the war with the French cost the king and the colonies a great deal of money. The king of England at that time was named George. He was an obstinate man, but not a very wise one, as you will think when you have learned more about him. One thing he wanted to do was to send soldiers to America to keep the French from getting back what they had lost, and he asked the people to pay these soldiers. He also asked them to send him money to pay the governors and judges whom he had chosen to rule over them. But the people thought they could take care of themselves, and did not want British soldiers. And they preferred to pay the governors and judges themselves as they had always done, and did not want King George to do it for them. So they would not send him the money he asked for.

Some of you may think this was very mean in the Americans, after all the British had done to help them in their war with the French. But they knew very well what they were about. They thought that if they gave the king a dollar today, he might want five dollars tomorrow and ten dollars the next day. They judged it best not to begin with the dollar. Kings, you should know, do not always make the best use of money that is given them by their people.

And that was not all. The people in the colonies did not like the way they had been treated by the English. They had mountains full of iron, but the king would not let them make this iron into tools. They had plenty of wool, but he would not let them weave it into cloth. They must buy these and other things in England, and must keep at farming; but they were not allowed to send their grain to England, but had to eat it all at home. They could not even send goods from one colony to another. Thus they were to be kept poor that the English merchants and manufacturers might grow rich.

These were some of the things the American people had to complain of. There were still other things, and a good many of the Americans had very little love for the English king and people. They felt that they were in a sort of slavery, and almost as if they had ropes on their hands and chains on their feet.

When King George was told that the Americans would not send him money, he was very angry. I am afraid he called them bad names. They were a low, ignorant, ungrateful set, he said, and he would show them who was their master. He would tax them and get money from them in that way. So the English Parliament, which is a body of lawmakers like our Congress, came together and passed laws to tax the Americans.

The first tax they laid is what is called a stamp tax. I fancy you know very well what that is, for we have a stamp tax in this country today. Everybody who sends away an express letter or package, has to buy a stamp from the government and put it on the envelope, and stamps have to be used on many other things.

But there is this difference. Our people are quite willing to buy these stamps, but they were not willing to buy the stamps which the British government sent them in 1765. Why? Well, they had a good reason for it, and this was that they had nothing to do with making the law. The English would not pay any taxes except those made by the people whom they elected to Parliament, and the Americans said they had the same right. They were not allowed to send any members to Parliament, so they said that Parliament had no right to tax them. Their own legislatures might vote to send the king money, but the English Parliament had no right to vote for them.

When the king found that the Americans would not use his stamps, he tried another plan. He laid a tax on tea and some other goods. He thought that our people could not do without tea, so he sent several shiploads across the ocean, expecting them to buy it and pay the tax. But he soon found that the colonists had no more use for taxed tea than for stamps. They would not even let the captains bring their tea on shore, except at Charleston, and there it was packed in damp cellars, where it soon rotted. A ship sent to Annapolis was set on fire and burned to the water's edge with the tea in it.

But the most stirring event took place at Boston. There one night, while the tea-ship lay at a wharf in the harbor, a number of young men dressed like Indians rushed on board with a loud war-whoop and began to break open the tea-chests with their hatchets and pour the tea into the harbor. This was the famous "Boston tea-party."

Americans like tea, but not tea with an English tax on it. They boiled leaves and roots and made some sort of tea out of them. It was poor stuff, but it did not pay any tax. And they would not buy any cloth or other goods brought from England. If the king was angry and stubborn, they were angry and stubborn too, and every day they grew more angry until many of them began to think that they would be better off without a king. They were not the kind of people to be made slaves of easily by King George or any other king.

When the king heard of the "Boston tea-party," he was in a fury. He would make Boston pay well for its tea, he said. So he sent soldiers there, and he gave orders that no ships should go into or out of Boston harbor. This stopped most of the business of the town, and soon the poor people had no work to do and very little to eat. But they had crowded meetings at Faneuil Hall, where Samuel Adams and John Hancock and other patriots talked to them of their rights and wrongs. It began to look as if war would soon come.

Chapter 17

The Shot Heard 'Round the World

The time had come at last for a union of the colonies. What Franklin had failed to do at Albany in 1754 was done in Philadelphia in 1774. A meeting was held there which was called a Congress, and was made up of some of the best men of the country sent from the colonies. One of these was George Washington, who had lived on his farm at Mt. Vernon since the end of the French and Indian War.

Congress sent a letter to the king, asking him to give the people of this country the same rights that the people of England had. There was no harm in this, I am sure, but it made the king more obstinate still. I have said he was not a wise man. Most people say he was a very foolish one, or he would have known that the people of the colonies would fight for their rights if they could not get them in peace.

All around Boston the farmers and villagers began to collect guns and powder and to drill men into soldiers. These were called "minute men," which meant that they would be ready to fight at a minute's notice, if they were asked to. When people begin to get ready in this way, war is usually not far off.

One night at Boston a man named Paul Revere stood watching a distant steeple till he saw a light suddenly flash out through the darkness. Then he leaped on his horse and rode at full speed away. That light was a signal telling him that British soldiers were on the march to Concord twenty miles away, to destroy some military stores which had been gathered there.

Away rode Revere through the night, rousing up the people and shouting to them that the British soldiers were coming. He was far ahead of the soldiers, so that when they reached the village of Lexington, ten miles from Boston, the people were wide awake, and a party of minute men was drawn up on the village green. The soldiers were ordered to fire on these men, and some of them fell dead. Those were the first shots in a great war. It was the 19th of April, 1775.

The British marched on to Concord, but the farmers had carried away most of the stores and buried them in the woods. Then the red-coats started back, and a terrible march they had of it. For all along the road were farmers with guns in their hands, firing on the troops from behind trees and stone walls. Some of the soldiers got back to Boston, but many of them lay dead in the road. The poor fellows killed at Lexington were terribly avenged.

Far and wide spread the news, and on all sides the farmers left their plows and took down their rifles, and thousands of them set out along the roads to Boston. Soon there were twenty thousand armed men around the town, and the British were shut up like rats in a trap. The American people were in rebellion against the king and war had begun.

It was to be a long and dreadful war, but it led to American liberty, and that was a thing well worth fighting for. While the people were laying siege to Boston, Congress was in session at Philadelphia, talking about what had best be done. One good thing they did was to make George Washington commander-in-chief of the army and send him to Boston to fight the British there. They could not have found a better soldier in all America.

The next good thing took place a year later. This was the thing which you celebrate with fireworks every 4th of July. Congress decided that this country ought to be free, and no longer to be under the rule of an English king. So a paper was written by a member from Virginia named Thomas Jefferson, with the help of Benjamin Franklin and some others. The paper is known by the long name of "Declaration of Independence." It declared that the American colonies were free from British rule, and in future would take care of themselves. It was on the 4th of July, 1776, that this great paper was adopted by Congress, and on that day the Republic of the United States of America was born. That is why our people have such a glad and noisy time every 4th of July.

Everywhere the people were full of joy when they heard what had been done. In the State House at Philadelphia rang out the great bell on which were the words "Proclaim liberty throughout the land and to all the inhabitants thereof." In New York the statue of King George was pulled down and thrown into the dust of the street. The people did not know what dark days lay before them, but they were ready to suffer much for the sake of liberty, and to risk all they had, life and all, for the freedom of their native land.

Paul Revere's Ride

Henry Wadsworth Longfellow

Listen, my children, and you shall hear
Of the midnight ride of Paul Revere,
On the eighteenth of April, in Seventy-five;
Hardly a man is now alive
Who remembers that famous day and year.

He said to his friend, "If the British march
By land or sea from the town tonight,
Hang a lantern aloft in the belfry arch
Of the North Church tower as a signal light—
One, if by land, and two, if by sea;
And I on the opposite shore will be,
Ready to ride and spread the alarm
Through every Middlesex village and farm,
For the country folk to be up and to arm."

Then he said, "Good-night!" and with muffled oar
Silently rowed to the Charlestown shore,
Just as the moon rose over the bay,
Where swinging wide at her moorings lay
The *Somerset*, British man-of-war;
A phantom ship, with each mast and spar
Across the moon like a prison bar,

And a huge black hulk, that was magnified
By its own reflection in the tide.

Meanwhile, his friend, through alley and street,
Wanders and watches, with eager ears,
Till in the silence around him he hears
The muster of men at the barrack door,
The sound of arms, and the tramp of feet,
And the measured tread of the grenadiers,
Marching down to their boats on the shore.

Then he climbed the tower of the Old North Church,
By the wooden stairs, with stealthy tread,
To the belfry-chamber overhead,
And startled the pigeons from their perch
On the somber rafters, that round him made
Masses and moving shapes of shade—
By the trembling ladder, steep and tall,
To the highest window in the wall,
Where he paused to listen and look down
A moment on the roofs of the town
And the moonlight flowing over all.

Beneath in the churchyard, lay the dead,
In their night-encampment on the hill,
Wrapped in silence so deep and still
That he could hear, like a sentinel's tread,
The watchful night-wind, as it went
Creeping along from tent to tent,
And seeming to whisper, "All is well!"
A moment only he feels the spell
Of the place and the hour, and the secret dread
Of the lonely belfry and the dead;
For suddenly all his thoughts are bent

On a shadowy something far away,
Where the river widens to meet the bay—
A line of black that bends and floats
On the rising tide, like a bridge of boats.

Meanwhile, impatient to mount and ride,
Booted and spurred, with a heavy stride
On the opposite shore walked Paul Revere.
Now he patted his horse's side,
Now gazed at the landscape far and near,
Then, impetuous, stamped the earth,
And turned and tightened his saddle girth;
But mostly he watched with eager search
The belfry tower of the Old North Church,
As it rose above the graves on the hill,
Lonely and spectral and somber and still.

And lo! as he looks, on the belfry's height
A glimmer, and then a gleam of light!
He springs to the saddle, the bridle he turns,
But lingers and gazes, till full on his sight
A second lamp in the belfry burns.

A hurry of hoofs in a village street,
A shape in the moonlight, a bulk in the dark,
And beneath, from the pebbles, in passing, a spark
Struck out by a steed flying fearless and fleet;
That was all! And yet, through the gloom and the light,
The fate of a nation was riding that night;
And the spark struck out by that steed, in his flight,
Kindled the land into flame with its heat.

He has left the village and mounted the steep,
And beneath him, tranquil and broad and deep,

Is the Mystic, meeting the ocean tides;
And under the alders that skirt its edge,
Now soft on the sand, now loud on the ledge,
Is heard the tramp of his steed as he rides.

It was twelve by the village clock
When he crossed the bridge into Medford town.
He heard the crowing of the cock,
And the barking of the farmer's dog,
And felt the damp of the river fog,
That rises after the sun goes down.
It was one by the village clock,
When he galloped into Lexington.
He saw the gilded weathercock
Swim in the moonlight as he passed,
And the meeting-house windows, blank and bare,
Gaze at him with a spectral glare,
As if they already stood aghast
At the bloody work they would look upon.

It was two by the village clock,
When he came to the bridge in Concord town.
He heard the bleating of the flock,
And the twitter of birds among the trees,
And felt the breath of the morning breeze
Blowing over the meadows brown.
And one was safe and asleep in his bed
Who at the bridge would be first to fall,
Who that day would be lying dead,
Pierced by a British musket-ball.

You know the rest. In the books you have read
How the British Regulars fired and fled—
How the farmers gave them ball for ball,

From behind each fence and farmyard wall,
Chasing the redcoats down the lane,
Then crossing the fields to emerge again
Under the trees at the turn of the road,
And only pausing to fire and load.

So through the night rode Paul Revere;
And so through the night went his cry of alarm
To every Middlesex village and farm—
A cry of defiance and not of fear,
A voice in the darkness, a knock at the door,
And a word that shall echo for evermore!
For, borne on the night-wind of the Past,
Through all our history, to the last,
In the hour of darkness and peril and need,
The people will awaken and listen to hear
The hurrying hoof-beats of that steed,
And the midnight message of Paul Revere.

Concord Hymn

Ralph Waldo Emerson

By the rude bridge that arched the flood,
　　Their flag to April's breeze unfurled,
Here once the embattled farmers stood,
　　And fired the shot heard round the world.

The foe long since in silence slept;
　　Alike the conqueror silent sleeps;
And Time the ruined bridge has swept
　　Down the dark stream which seaward creeps.

On this green bank, by this soft stream,
　　We set today a votive stone;
That memory may their deed redeem,
　　When, like our sires, our sons are gone.

Spirit, that made those heroes dare
　　To die, and leave their children free,
Bid Time and Nature gently spare
　　The shaft we raise to them and thee.

Chapter 18

Fighting for Freedom

Any of my readers who are true, sound-hearted Americans, and I am sure all of them are that, would have been glad to see how the New England farmers swarmed around Boston in April, 1775. Some of them had fought in the French war, and brought with them their rusty old muskets, which they knew very well how to use. And most of them were hunters and had learned how to shoot. And all of them were bold and brave and were determined to have a free country. The English red-coat soldiers in Boston would soon find that these countrymen were not men to be laughed at, even if they had not been trained in war.

One morning the English woke up and rubbed their eyes hard, for there, on a hill that overlooked the town, was a crowd of Americans. They had been at work all night, digging and making earthworks to fight behind, and now had quite a fort. The English officers did not like the look of things, for the Americans could fire from Breeds Hill (though they called it the Battle of Bunker Hill) straight down into the town. They must be driven away or they would drive the troops away.

I can tell you that was a busy and a bloody day for Boston. The great war-ships in the harbor thundered with their cannon at the men on the hill. And the soldiers began to march up the hill, thinking that the Yankees would run like sheep when they saw the red-coats coming near. But the Yankees were not there to run.

"Don't fire, boys, till you see the whites of their eyes," said brave General Prescott.

So the Yankee boys waited till the British were close at hand. Then they fired and the red-coats fell in rows, for the farmers did not waste their bullets. Those that did not fall scampered in haste down the hill. It was a strange sight to see British soldiers running away from Yankee farmers.

After awhile the British came again. They were not so sure this time. Again the Yankee muskets rattled along the earthworks, and again the British turned and ran—those who were able to.

They could never have taken that hill if the farmer soldiers had not run out of powder. When the red-coats came a third time, the Yankees could not fire and had to fight them with the butts of their guns. So the British won the hill; but they had found that the Yankee farmers were not cowards; after that time they never liked to march against American earthworks.

Not long after the Battle of Bunker Hill, General Washington came to command the Americans, and he spent months in drilling and making soldiers out of them. He also got a good supply of powder and muskets and some cannon, and one dark night in March, 1776, he built a fort on another hill that looked down on Boston.

I warrant you, the British were scared when they looked up that hill the next morning and saw cannon on its top and men behind the cannon. They would have to climb that hill as they had done Breeds Hill, or else leave Boston. But they had no fancy for another Bunker Hill, so they decided to leave. They got on their ships and sailed away, and Washington and his men marched joyfully into the town. That was a great day for America, and it was soon followed by the 4th of July and the glorious Declaration of Independence. Since that 4th of July, no king has ever ruled over the United States.

We call this war the American Revolution. Do you know what a revolution is? It means the doing away with a bad government and replacing it with a better one. In this country it meant that our people were tired of the rule of England and wished to govern themselves. They had to fight hard for their freedom, it is true, but it was well worth fighting for.

The war was a long and dreadful one. It went on for seven long years. At one time everything seemed lost; at other times all grew bright and hopeful. And thus it went on, up and down, to the end. I cannot tell you all that took place, but I will give you the important points.

After the British left Boston, they sailed about for a time, and then they came with a large army to New York. Washington was there with his soldiers to meet them, and did his best, but everything seemed to go wrong. First, the Americans were beaten in battle and had to march out of New York and let the British march in. Then Washington and his ragged men were obliged to hasten across the state of New Jersey with a strong British force after them. They were too weak to face the British.

When they got to the Delaware River, the Americans crossed it and took all the boats, so that the British could not follow them. It was now near winter time, and both armies went into winter quarters. They faced each other, but the wide river ran between.

You may well think that by this time the American people were getting very down-hearted. Many of them thought that all was lost, and that they would have to submit to King George. The army dwindled away and no new soldiers came in, so that it looked as if it would go to pieces. It was growing very dark for American liberty..

But there was one man who did not despair, and that man was George Washington. He saw that something must be done to stir up the spirits of the people, and he was just the man to do it. It was a wonderful Christmas he kept that year. All Christmas day his ragged and hungry soldiers were marching up their side of the Delaware and crossing the river in boats, though the wind was biting cold, and the air was full of falling snow, and the broken ice was floating in great blocks down the river; but nothing stopped the gallant soldiers. All Christmas night they marched down the other side of the river, though their shoes were so bad that the ground became reddened by blood from their feet. Two of the poor fellows were frozen to death.

At Trenton, a number of miles below, there was a body of German soldiers. These had been hired by King George to help him fight his battles. That day they had been eating a good Christmas dinner while the hungry Americans were marching through the snow. At night they went to bed, not dreaming of danger.

They were wakened in the morning by shots and shouts. Washington and his men were in the streets of the town. They had hardly time to seize their guns before the ragged Yankees were all around them, and nearly all of them were made prisoners of war.

Was not that a great and glorious deed? It filled the Americans with new hope. In a few days afterwards, Washington defeated the British in another battle, and then settled down with his ragged but brave men in the hills of New Jersey. He did not go behind a river this time. The British knew where he was and could come to see him if they wanted to. But they did not come. Very likely they had seen enough of him for that winter.

Chapter 19

Valley Forge and Dark Days

The next year things went wrong again for Washington. A large British army sailed from New York and landed at the head of Chesapeake Bay. Then they marched overland to Philadelphia. Washington fought a battle with them on Brandywine Creek, but his men were defeated and the British marched on and entered Philadelphia. They now held the largest cities of the country, Philadelphia and New York.

While the British were living in plenty and having a very good time in the Quaker city, the poor Americans spent a wretched and terrible winter at a place called Valley Forge. The winter was a dismally cold one, and the men had not half enough food to eat or clothes to wear, and very poor huts to live in. They suffered dreadfully, and before the spring came, many of them died from disease and exposure.

Poor fellows! they were paying dearly for their struggle for liberty. But there was no such despair this winter as there had been the winter before, for news came from the north that warmed the soldiers up like a fire. Though Washington had lost a battle, a great victory had been gained by the Americans at Saratoga, in the upper part of New York state.

While General Howe was marching on Philadelphia, another British army, under General Burgoyne, had been marching south from Canada, along the line of Lake Champlain and Lake George.

But Burgoyne and his men soon found themselves in a tight place. Food began to run short and a regiment of a thousand men was sent into Vermont to seize some stores. They were met by the Green Mountain boys, led by Colonel Stark, a brave old soldier.

"There are the red-coats," said the bold colonel. "We must beat them today, or Betty Stark is a widow."

Beat them they did. Only seventy men got back to Burgoyne. All the rest were killed or captured.

Another force, under Colonel St. Leger, marched south from Oswego, on Lake Ontario. A large body of Indians was with him. This army stopped to besiege a fort in the wilderness, and General Arnold marched to relieve the fort.

The way Arnold defeated St. Leger was a very curious one. He sent a half-witted fellow into the Indian camp with the tale that a great American force was coming. The messenger came running in among the savages with bullet-holes in his clothes. He seemed half scared to death, and told the Indians that a vast host was coming after him as thick as the leaves on the trees.

This story frightened the Indians and they ran off in great haste through the woods. When the British soldiers saw this, they fell into such a panic that they took to their heels, leaving all their tents and cannon behind them. The people in the fort did not know what it meant, till Arnold came up and told them how he had won a victory without firing a shot.

All this was very bad for Burgoyne. The Indians he brought with him began to leave. At length he found himself in a terrible plight. His provisions were nearly gone, he was surrounded by the Americans, and after fighting two battles he retreated to Saratoga. Here he had to surrender. He and all his army became prisoners to the Americans.

We cannot wonder that this warmed up the Americans like a fire. It filled the English with despair. They began to think that they would never win back the colonies.

One thing the good news did was to get the French to come

to the help of the Americans. Benjamin Franklin was then in Paris, and he asked the king to send ships and men and money to America. The French had no love for the British, who had taken from them all their colonies in America, so they did as Franklin wished.

There are two more things I wish to tell you in this chapter, one good and one bad. When the British in Philadelphia heard that the French were coming to help the Americans, they were afraid they might be caught in a trap. So they left in great haste and marched for New York. Washington followed and fought a battle with them, but they got away. After that Washington's army laid siege to New York, as it had formerly done to Boston.

That was the good thing. The bad thing was this. General Benedict Arnold, who had defeated St. Leger and his Indians, and who was one of the bravest of the American officers, turned traitor to his country. He had charge of West Point, a strong fort on the Hudson River, and tried to give this up to the British. But he was found out and had to flee for his life. Major Andre, a British officer, who had been sent to talk with Arnold, was caught by three American scouts on his way back to New York. They searched him for papers, and found what they wanted hidden in his boot. Poor Andre was hung for a spy, but the traitor Arnold escaped. But he was hated by the Americans and despised by the British, and twenty years afterwards he died in shame and remorse.

Chapter 20

John Paul Jones,
Naval Hero of the Revolution

We are justly proud of our great war-ships, with their strong steel sides and their mighty guns, which can fire missiles at targets miles away.

Such ships and such guns as these had not been dreamed of in the days of the Revolution. Then there were only small wooden vessels, moved by sails instead of engines, and a cannonball that weighed twenty-four pounds was thought very heavy. Six- and twelve-pound cannonballs were common. And to hit a ship a mile away! It was not to be thought of. I tell you, in those days ships had to fight nearly side by side and men to fight face to face. To be a mile away was as good as being a hundred miles.

But for all this there was some hard fighting done at sea in the Revolutionary War, in spite of the small ships and little guns. They fought closer together, that was all. Boast as we may about the wonderful work done by our ships lately, we have just as much right to be proud of the deeds of our great naval hero of the Revolutionary War, with his rotten old ship and poor little guns, but with his stout heart behind them all.

This hero was the sturdy John Paul Jones, one of the boldest and bravest men that ever stood on a ship's deck. And his great sea fight has had nothing to surpass it in all the history of naval war. I cannot tell you the story of the Revolution without telling about the great ocean victory of the bold-hearted John Paul Jones.

Poor ships enough we had to fight with. A little fleet of seven or eight small vessels, whose heaviest guns threw only nine-pound cannonballs, and the most of them only six-pound. You could have thrown these yourself with one hand, though not so far. These were all we had at first to fight more than seventy British ships, with guns that threw eighteen-pound cannonballs, and some still heavier. Do you not think it looked like a one-sided fight?

But the Americans had one great advantage. They had not many merchant ships and not much to lose upon the seas. On the other hand, the ocean swarmed with the merchant ships of England, and with the store ships bringing supplies of guns and powder and food to the armies on shore. Here were splendid prizes for our gallant seamen, and out of every port sailed bold privateers, sweeping the seas and bringing in many a richly-laden craft.

Some of the best fighting of the war was done by these privateers. While they were hunting for merchant ships, they often came across war-ships, and you can be sure they did not always run away. No, indeed; they were usually ready to fight, and during the war no less than sixteen war vessels were captured by our ocean rovers. On the other hand, the British privateers did not capture a single American war-ship. As for merchant vessels, our privateers brought them in by the dozens. One fleet of sixty vessels set out from Ireland for the West Indies, and out of these, thirty-five were gobbled up by our privateers, and their rich stores brought into American ports. During the whole war, the privateers took more than seven hundred prizes. I might go on to tell you of some of their hard fights, but I think you would rather read the story of John Paul Jones, the boldest and bravest of them all, the terror of the seas to the British fleet.

John Paul Jones, you should know, was born in Scotland. But he made America his home. And as he was known to be a good sailor, he was appointed first lieutenant of the *Alfred,* the flagship of our small fleet. He had the honor to be the first man to raise a flag on an American man-of-war, and that is something to be proud of. This took place on the Delaware, at Philadelphia, about Christmas, 1775.

It was an important ceremony, for the fleet was just being put in commission. At a given signal Lieutenant Jones grasped the halyards and hauled up to the mizzen topmast a great flag of yellow silk. As it unfurled to the breeze, cannon roared and crowds on the shore lustily cheered. In the centre of the flag was seen the figure of a green pine tree, and under this a rattlesnake lay coiled, with the warning motto, "Don't tread on me!"

This was the famous rattlesnake flag. Another flag was raised on which were thirteen stripes, alternately red and white, and in the corner the British union jack. We then had the stripes but not the stars. They were to come after the Declaration of Independence and the union of the states.

In August, 1776, Congress made Paul Jones captain of the brig *Providence,* and he soon showed what kind of a man he was. He came across a fleet of five vessels, and made up his mind to capture the largest of them, which he thought to be a fine merchant ship. He got pretty close up before he learned his mistake. It was the British frigate *Solebay,* strong enough to make mince-meat of his little brig. There was nothing for it but to run, and Captain Jones made haste to get away, followed by the *Solebay.* But the Briton gained on the American, and after a four-hours' run, the frigate was less than a hundred yards away. It might at any minute sink the daring little *Providence* by a broadside.

But Paul Jones was not the man to be caught. Suddenly the helm of the brig was put hard up, as sailors say, and the little craft turned and dashed across the frigate's bow. As it did so the flag of the republic was spread to the breeze, and a broadside from the brig's guns swept the frigate's deck. Then, with all sail set, away dashed the *Providence* before the breeze. As soon as the British got back their senses, they fired all their guns at the brig. But not a ball hit her, and with the best of the wind, she soon left the *Solebay* far behind.

And now I must tell the story of John Paul Jones' greatest fight. In its way, it was the greatest sea-fight ever seen. It was fought with a fleet in which Jones sailed from a French port, for Congress had found what a hero they had in their Scotch sailor, and now they made him commodore of a fleet.

The flagship of this fleet was a rotten old log of a ship, which had sailed in the East India merchant service till its timbers were in a state of dry rot. It was a shapeless tub of a vessel, better fitted to lie in port and keep rabbits in than to send out as a battle-ship. John Paul Jones named it the *Bon Homme Richard,* which, in English means "Poor Richard." This was a name used by Benjamin Franklin for his almanac.

It was not until the summer of 1779 that Jones was able to set sail. His ship had thirty-six guns, such as they were, and he had with him three consorts under French officers—the *Alliance,* the *Pallas,* and the *Vengeance.* Among this crew were a hundred American sailors, who had just been set free from English prisons. And his master's mate, Richard Dale, a man of his own sort, had just escaped from prison in England.

Away they went, east and west, north and south, around the British Isles, seeking for the men-of-war which should have swarmed in those seas, but finding only merchant vessels, a number of which were captured and their crews kept as prisoners. But the gallant commodore soon got tired of this. He had come out to fight, and he wanted to find something worth fighting. At length, on September 23rd, he came in view of a large fleet of merchant ships, forty-two in all, under the charge of two frigates, the *Serapis,* of forty-two guns, and the *Countess of Scarborough,* of twenty-two smaller guns.

Commodore Jones left the smaller vessel for his consorts to deal with, and dashed away for the *Serapis* as fast as the tub-like *Bon Homme Richard* could go. The British ship was much stronger than his in number and weight of guns, but he cared very little for that. The *Serapis* had ten 18-pound cannon in each battery, and the *Bon Homme Richard* only three. And these were such sorry excuses for cannon that two of them burst at the first fire, killing and wounding the most of their crews. After that Jones did all his fighting with 12- and 8-pound guns; that is, with guns which fired balls of these weights.

It was night when the battle began. Soon the 18-pounders of the *Serapis* were playing havoc with the sides of the *Bon Homme Richard*. Many of the balls went clear through her and plunged into the sea beyond. Some struck her below the water level, and soon the rotten old craft was "leaking like a basket."

It began to look desperate for Jones and his ship. He could not half reply to the heavy fire of the English guns, and great chasms were made in the ship's side, where the 18-pound balls tore out the timbers between the port holes.

Captain Pearson of the *Serapis* looked at his staggering and leaking antagonist, and thought it about time for the battle to end.

"Have you surrendered?" he shouted across the water to Commodore Jones.

"I have not yet begun to fight," was the famous answer of the brave John Paul Jones.

Surrender, indeed! I doubt if that word was in John Paul Jones' dictionary. He would rather have let his vessel sink. The ships now drifted together, and by Jones' order the jib-boom of the *Serapis* was lashed to his mizzen-mast. This brought the ships so close side by side that the English gunners could not open their ports, and had to fire through them and blow them off. And the gunners on both sides had to thrust the handles of their rammers through the enemy's port holes, in order to load their guns.

Affairs were now desperate. The *Bon Homme Richard* was on fire in several places. Water was pouring into her through a dozen rents. It seemed as if she must sink or burn. Almost any man except John Paul Jones would have given up the fight. I know I should, and I fancy most of you would have done the same. But there was no give up in that man's soul.

One would think that nothing could have been worse, but worse still was to come. In this crisis the *Alliance,* one of Jones' small fleet, came up and fired two broadsides into the wounded flag-ship, killing a number of her crew. Whether this was done on purpose or by mistake is not known. The French captain did not like Commodore Jones, and most men think he played the traitor.

And another bad thing took place. There were two or three hundred English prisoners on the *Bon Homme Richard,* taken from her prizes. One of the American officers, thinking that all was over, set these men free, and they came swarming up. At the same time one of the crew tried to haul down the flag and cried to the British for quarter. Paul Jones knocked him down by flinging a pistol at his head. He might sink or burn—but give up the ship? never!

The tide of change now began to turn. Richard Dale, the master's mate, told the English prisoners that the vessel was sinking, and set them at work pumping and fighting the fire to save their lives. And one of the marines, who was fighting on the yard-arms, dropped a hand grenade into the open hatch of the *Serapis.* It set fire to a heap of gun cartridges that lay below, and these exploded, killing twenty of the gunners and wounding many more, while the ship was set on fire. This ended the fight. The fire of the marines from the mast-tops had cleared the decks of the *Serapis* of men. Commodore Jones aided in this with the 9-pounders on his deck, loading and firing them himself. Captain Pearson stood alone, and when he heard the roar of the explosion, he could bear the strain no longer. He ran and pulled down the flag, which had been nailed to the mast.

"Cease firing," said John Paul Jones.

The *Serapis* was his. Well and nobly had it been won.

Never had there been a victory gained in such straits. The *Bon Homme Richard* was fast settling down into the sea. Pump as they would, they could not save her. Inch by inch she sank deeper. Jones and his gallant crew boarded the *Serapis,* and at nine o'clock the next morning the noble old craft sank beneath the ocean waves, laden with honor, and with her victorious flag still flying. The *Serapis* was brought safely into port.

Captain Pearson had fought bravely, and the British ministry made him a knight for his courage.

"If I had a chance to fight him again I would make him a lord," said brave John Paul Jones.

Never before or since has a victory been won under such desperate circumstances as those of John Paul Jones, with his sinking and burning ship, his bursting guns, his escaped prisoners, and his treacherous consort. It was a victory to put his name forever on the annals of fame.

Chapter 21
Marion, the Swamp Fox

Far away back in old English history there was a famous archer named Robin Hood, who lived in the deep woods with a bold band of outlaws like himself. He and his band were foes of the nobles and friends of the poor, and his name will never be forgotten by the people of England.

No doubt you have read about the gallant archer. No man of his time could send an arrow so straight and sure as he. But we need not go back for hundreds of years to find our Robin Hood. We have had a man like him in our own country, who fought for us in the Revolution. His name was Francis Marion, and he was known as the "Swamp Fox"; for he lived in the swamps of South Carolina as Robin Hood did in the forests of England, and he was the stinging foe of the oppressors of the people.

I have already told you about the war in the North, and of how the British, after doing all they could to overthrow Washington and conquer the country, found themselves shut up in the city of New York, with Washington like a watch-dog outside.

When the British generals found that the North was too hard a nut to crack, they thought they would try what they could do in the South. So they sent a fleet and an army down the coast, and before long they had taken the cities of Savannah and Charleston, and had their soldiers marching all over Georgia and South Carolina. General Gates, the man to whom Burgoyne surrendered, came down with a force of militia to fight them, but he was beaten so badly that he had to run away without a soldier to follow him. You can imagine that the British were proud of their success. They thought themselves masters of the South, and fancied they had only to march north and become masters there, too.

But you must not think that they were quite masters. Back in the woods and the swamps were men with arms in their hands and with patriotism in their hearts. They were like wasps or hornets, who kept darting out from their nests, stinging the British troops, and then darting back out of sight. These gallant bands were led by Marion, Sumter, Pickens, and other brave men; but Marion's band was the most famous of them all, so I shall tell you about the Swamp Fox and what he did.

I fancy all of my young friends would have laughed if they had seen Marion's band when it joined General Gates' army. Such scarecrows of soldiers they were! There were only about twenty of them in all, some of them white and some black, some men and some boys, dressed in rags that fluttered in the wind, and on horses that looked as if they had been fed on corn-cobs instead of corn.

Gates and his men did laugh at them, though they took care not to laugh when Marion was at hand. He was a small man, with a thin face, and dressed not much better than his men. But there was a look in his eye that told the soldiers he was not a safe man to laugh at.

Marion and his men were soon off again on a scout, and after Gates and his army had been beaten and scattered to the winds, they went back to their hiding places in the swamps to play the hornet once more.

Along the Pedee River these swamps extended for miles. There were islands of dry land far within, but they could only be reached by narrow paths which the British were not able to find. Only men who had spent their lives in that country could make their way safely through this broad stretch of water plants and water-soaked ground.

Marion's force kept changing. Now it went down to twenty men, now up to a hundred or more. It was never large, for there was not food or shelter for many men. But there were enough of them to give the British plenty of trouble. They had their sentries on the outlook, and when a party of British or Tories went carelessly past, out would spring Marion's men, send their foes flying like deer, and then back they would go before a strong body of the enemy could reach them.

These brave fellows had many hiding places in the swamps and many paths out of them. Today they might strike the British in one place and tomorrow in another many miles away. Small as their force was, they gave the enemy far more trouble than Gates had done with all his army. Marion's headquarters was a tract of land known as Snow's Island, where a creek ran into the Pedee. It was high and dry, was covered with trees and thickets, and was full of game. And all around it spread the soaking swamp, with paths known only to the patriot band. Among all their hiding places, this was their chosen home.

You may be sure that the British did their best to capture a man who gave them so much trouble as Marion. They sent Colonel Wemyss, one of their best cavalry officers, to hunt him down. Marion was then far from his hiding place and Wemyss got on his trail. But the Swamp Fox was hard to catch. He led the British a lively chase, and when they gave it up in despair, he followed them back. He came upon a large body of Tories and struck them so suddenly that hardly a man of them escaped, while he lost only one man. Tories, you should know, were Americans who fought on the British side.

The next man who tried to capture Marion was Colonel Tarleton, a hard rider and a good soldier, but a cruel and brutal man. He was hated in the South as much as Benedict Arnold was in the North. There is a good story told about how he was tricked by one of Marion's men. One day as he and his men were riding furiously along, they came up to an old farmer, who was hoeing in his field beside the road.

"Can you tell me what became of the man who galloped by here just ahead of us?" asked one of them. "I will give you fifty pounds if you put me on his track."

"Do you mean the man on a black horse with a white star in its forehead?" asked the farmer.

"Yes, that's the fellow."

"He looked to me like Jack Davis, one of Marion's men, but he went past so fast that I could not be sure."

"Never mind who he was. What we want to know is where to find him."

"Bless your heart! he was going at such a pace that he couldn't well stop under four or five miles. I'm much afeard I can't earn that fifty pounds."

On rode the troop, and back into the woods went the farmer. He had not gone far before he came to a black horse with a white star in its forehead. This he mounted and rode away. The farmer was Jack Davis himself.

That was the kind of men Tarleton had to deal with, and you may be sure that he did not catch any of them. He had his hunt, but he caught no game.

Chapter 22

General Greene

While Marion was keeping the war alive in South Carolina, an army was gathering under General Greene, who was, next to Washington, the best of the American generals. With him were Daniel Morgan, a famous leader of riflemen, William Washington, a cousin of the commander-in-chief, and Henry Lee, or "Light-horse Harry," father of the famous General Lee of the Civil War.

General Greene got together about two thousand men, half armed and half supplied and knowing nothing about war, so that he had a poor chance of defeating the trained British soldiers. But he was a Marion on a larger scale, and knew when to retreat and when to advance. I must tell you what he did.

In the first place Morgan the rifleman met the bold Colonel Tarleton and gave him a sound flogging. Tarleton hurried back to Lord Cornwallis, the British commander in the South. Cornwallis thought he would catch Morgan napping, but the lively rifleman was too wide-awake for him. He hurried back with the prisoners he had taken from Tarleton, and crossed the Catawba River just as the British came up. That night it rained hard, and the river rose so that it could not be crossed for three days.

General Greene now joined Morgan, and the retreat continued to the Yadkin River. This, too, was crossed by the Americans and rain again came up and swelled the river before the British could follow. When the British got across, there was a race for the Dan River on the borders of Virginia. Green got there first, crossed the stream, and held the fords against the foe. Cornwallis by this time had enough of it. Provisions were growing scarce, and he turned back. But he soon had Greene on his track, and he did not find his march a very comfortable one.

Here I must tell you an interesting anecdote about General Greene. Once, during his campaign, he entered a tavern at Salisbury, in North Carolina. He was wet to the skin from a heavy rain. Steele, the landlord, knew him and looked at him in surprise.

"Why, general, you are not alone?" he asked.

"Yes," said the general, "here I am, all alone, very tired, hungry, and penniless."

Mrs. Steele hastened to set a smoking hot meal before the hungry traveler. Then, while he was eating, she drew from under her apron two bags of silver and laid them on the table before him.

"Take these, general," she said. "You need them and I can do without them."

You may see that the women as well as the men of America did all they could for liberty, for there were many others like Mrs. Steele.

I have told you that General Greene was one of the ablest of the American leaders, and you have seen how he got the best of Cornwallis in the retreat. Several times afterwards he fought with the British. He was always defeated. His country soldiers could not face the British veterans. But each time he managed to get as much good from the fight as if he had a victory, and by the end of the year the British were shut up in Charleston and Savannah, and the South was free again.

Where was Cornwallis during this time? Greene had led him so far north that he concluded to march on into Virginia and get the troops he would find there, and then come back. There was fighting going on in Virginia at this time. General Arnold, the traitor, was there, fighting against his own people. Against him was General Lafayette, a young French nobleman who had come to the help of the Americans.

I suppose some of you have read stories of how a wolf or some other wild animal walked into a trap, from which it could not get out again. Lord Cornwallis was not a wild animal, but he walked into just such a trap after he got to Virginia. When he reached there, he took command of Arnold's troops. But he found himself not yet strong enough to face Lafayette, so he marched to Yorktown, near the mouth of York River, where he expected to get help by sea from New York. Yorktown was the trap he walked into, as you will see.

France had sent a fleet and an army to help the Americans, and just then this fleet came up from the West Indies and sailed into the Chesapeake, shutting off Yorktown from the sea. At the same time Washington, who had been closely watching what was going on, broke camp before New York and marched southward as fast as his men could go. Before Cornwallis could guess what was about to happen, the trap was closed on him. In the bay near Yorktown was the strong French fleet; before Yorktown was the army of American and French soldiers.

There was no escape. The army and the fleet bombarded the town. A week of this was enough for Lord Cornwallis. He surrendered his army, seven thousand strong, on October 19, 1781, and the war was at an end. America was free.

Chapter 23
The Voyage of Our Ship of State

Have any of my young readers ever been to Europe? Likely enough some of you may have been, for even young folks cross the ocean now-a-days. It has got to be an easy journey, with swift ships and jet airplanes. But in past times it was a long and difficult journey, in which the ship was often tossed by terrible storms, and sometimes was broken to pieces on the rocks or went to the bottom with all on board.

What I wish to say is, that those who come from Europe to this country leave countries that are governed by kings and come to a country that is governed by the people. In some of the countries of Europe the people might as well be slaves, for they have no vote and no one to speak for them, and the man who rules them is born to power. Even in England, which is the freest of them all, there is a king or queen and a House of Lords who are born to power. The people can vote, but only for members of the House of Commons. They have nothing to do with the monarch or the Lords.

Of course you all know that this is not the case in our country. Here every man in power is put there by the votes of the people. As President Lincoln said, we have a government "of the people, by the people, and for the people."

We did not have such a government before the 4th of July, 1776. Our country was then governed by a king, and, what was worse, this king was on the other side of the ocean, and cared nothing for the people of America except as money bags to fill his purse. But after that 4th of July, we governed ourselves, and had no king for lord and master; and we have got along very well without one.

Now you can see what the Declaration of Independence and the Revolution meant. With the Declaration, we cut loose from England. Our Ship of State set out on its long voyage to liberty. The Declaration cut the chain that fastened this great ship to England's shores. The Revolution was like the stormy passage across the ocean waves. At times it looked as if our Ship of State would be torn to pieces by the storms, or driven back to the shores from which it set sail; but then the clouds would break and the sun shine, and onward our good ship would speed. At length it reached the port of liberty, and came to anchor far away from the land of kings.

This is a sort of parable. I think every one of you will know what it means. The people of this country had enough of kings and their ways, and of being taxed without their consent. They determined to be free to tax and govern themselves. It was for this they fought in the Revolution, and they won liberty with their blood.

And now, before we go on with the history of our country, it will be wise to stop and ask what kind of government the Americans gave themselves. They had thrown overboard the old government of kings. They had to make a new government of the people. I hope you do not think this was an easy task. If an architect or builder is shown a house and told to build another like that, he finds it very easy to do. But if he is shown a heap of stone and bricks and wood and told to build out of them a good strong house unlike any he has ever seen, he will find his task a very hard one, and may spoil the house in his building.

That was what our people had to do. They could have built a king's government easily enough. They had plenty of patterns to follow for that. But they had no pattern for a people's government, and, like the architect and his house, they might spoil it in the making. The fact is, this is just what they did. Their first government was spoiled in the making, and they had to take it down and build it over again.

This was done by what we call a Convention, made up of delegates sent by the several states. The Convention met in Philadelphia in 1787 for the purpose of forming a Constitution; that is, a plan of government under which the people should live and which the states and their citizens should have to obey.

This Convention was a wonderful body of statesmen. Its like has not often been seen. The wisest and ablest men of all the states were sent to it. They included all the great men—some we know already, Washington, Franklin, Jefferson, and Adams, and many others of fine ability. For four months these men worked in secret. It was a severe task they had to perform, for some wanted one thing and some another, and many times it looked as if they would never agree; but at length all disputes were settled and their long labors were at an end.

General Washington was president of the Convention, and back of the chair on which he sat, the figure of the sun was painted on the wall. When it was all over, Benjamin Franklin pointed to this painting and said to those who stood near him:

"Often while we sat here, troubled by hopes and fears, I have looked towards that figure and asked myself if it was a rising or a setting sun. Now I know that it is the rising sun."

The rising sun indeed it was, for when the Convention had finished its work, it had formed the noble Constitution under which we now live, the greatest state paper which man has ever formed.

But I fancy you want to know more about the noble framework of government built by the wise men of the Convention of 1787.

After the Union was formed, there were thirteen states still, but each of these had lost some of its old powers. The powers taken from the states were given to the general government. Every state had still the right to manage its own affairs, but such things as concerned the whole people were managed by the general government.

What were these things? Let us see. There was the power to coin money, to lay taxes, to control the post-office, and to make laws for the good of the whole nation. And there was the power to form an army and navy, to make treaties with other countries, and to declare war if we could not get on in peace.

Under the Confederation which was formed during the Revolutionary War, the states could do these things for themselves; under the Constitution they could do none of these things, but they could pass laws that affected only themselves, and could tax their own people for state purposes.

I have spoken several times of the general government. No doubt you wish to know what this government was like. Well, it consisted of three bodies, one of which made laws for the people, the second considered if these laws agreed with the Constitution, the third executed these laws, or put them in force.

The body that made the laws was named the Congress of the United States. It consisted of two sections. One was called the Senate and was made up of two members from each state. The other section was called the House of Representatives, and its members were directly voted for by the people. The members of the Senate were voted for by the legislatures of the states, who had been elected by the people.

All the laws were to be made by Congress, but not one of them could become a law until approved by the President. If he did not approve of any law, he vetoed it, or returned it without being signed with his name, and then it could not be enforced as a law until voted for by two-thirds of the members of Congress.

It was the duty of the President to execute the laws. He took the place of the kings in other countries. But he was not born to his position like a king, but had to be voted for by the people, and could only stay in office for four years. Then he, or some one else, had to be voted for again.

Next to the President was the Vice-President, who was to take his place if he should die or resign. While the President was in office, the Vice-President had nothing to do except to act as presiding officer of the Senate. What we call the Cabinet are persons chosen by the President to help him in his work. You must understand that it takes a number of leading men and a great many under men to do all the work of the head of our government.

The third body of our government was called the Supreme Court. This was made up of some of the ablest lawyers and judges of the country. They were not to be voted for, but to be chosen by the President. The duty of the Supreme Court is to consider any law brought to its notice and decide if it agrees with the Constitution. If the Court decides that a law is not constitutional, it ceases to be of any effect.

This is not so very hard to understand, is it? The President and Congress elected by the people; the Supreme Court and Cabinet selected by the President; the Constitution the foundation of our government; and the laws passed by Congress, the edifice erected on the foundation.

Its great feature is that it is a republic—a government "of the people, by the people, and for the people." Ours is not the first republic. There have been others. But it is the greatest. It is the only one that covers half a continent and is made up of states, many of which are larger than some of the kingdoms of Europe. For more than two hundred years the Constitution made in 1787 has held good. Then it covered thirteen states and less than four million people; now it covers fifty states and more than 300 million people.

Sail On, O Ship of State!

from *The Building of the Ship*
Henry Wadsworth Longfellow

Thou, too, sail on, O Ship of State!
 Sail on, O Union, strong and great!
Humanity with all its fears,
With all its hopes of future years,
Is hanging breathless on thy fate!
We know what Master laid thy keel,
What Workmen wrought thy ribs of steel,
Who made each mast, and sail, and rope,
What anvils rang, what hammers beat,
In what a forge and what a heat
Were shaped the anchors of thy hope!
Fear not each sudden sound and shock,
'Tis of the wave and not the rock;
'Tis but the flapping of the sail,
And not a rent made by a gale!
In spite of rock and tempest's roar,
In spite of false lights on the shore,
Sail on, nor fear to breast the sea!
Our hearts, our hopes, are all with thee,
Our hearts, our hopes, our prayers, our tears,
Our faith triumphant o'er our fears,
Are all with thee,—are all with thee!

Chapter 24
President Washington

E very four years a great question arises in this country, and all the States and their people are disturbed until this question is settled. Even business nearly stops still, for many persons can think of nothing but the answer to this question.

Who shall be President? That is the question which, at the end of every four years, troubles the minds of our people. This question was asked for the first time in 1788, after the Constitution had been made and accepted by the States, but this time the people found it a very easy question to answer.

There were several men who had taken a great part in the making of our country, and who might have been named for President. One of these was Thomas Jefferson, who wrote the Declaration of Independence. Another of them was Benjamin Franklin, who got France to come to our aid and did many other noble things for his country. But none of them stood so high in the respect and admiration of the people as George Washington, who had led our armies through the great war, and to whom, more than to any other man, we owed our liberty.

This time, then, there was no real question as to who should be President. Washington was the man. All men, all parties, settled upon Washington. No one opposed him; there was no man in the country like him. He was unanimously elected the first President of the United States.

In olden times, when a victorious general came back to Rome with the splendid spoils brought from distant countries, the people gave him a triumph, and all Rome rose to do him honor and to gaze upon the splendor of the show. Washington had no splendid spoils to display. But he had the love of the people, which was far better than gold and silver won in war; and all the way from his home at Mount Vernon to New York, where he was to take the office of President, the people honored him with a triumph.

Along the whole journey men, women, and children crowded the roadside and waited for hours to see him pass. That was before the day of railroads or automobiles or airplanes, and he had to go slowly in his carriage, so that everybody had a fine chance to see and greet him as he went by. Guns were fired as he passed through the towns; arches of triumph were erected for his carriage to go under; flowers were strewn in the streets for its wheels to roll over; cheers and cries of greeting filled the air; all that the people could do to honor their great hero was done.

On the 30th of April, 1789, Washington took the oath of office as the first President of our country and people. He stood on the balcony of a building in front of Federal Hall, in which Congress met, and in the street before him was a vast multitude, full of joy and hope. When he had taken the oath, cannon roared out, bells were rung in all the neighboring steeples, and a mighty shout burst from the assembled multitude:

"Long live George Washington, President of the United States!"

This, as I have said, was in New York. But Philadelphia was soon chosen as the seat of government, and the President and Congress moved to that city the next year. There they stayed for ten years. In the year 1800 a new city, named Washington, on the banks of the Potomac, was made the capital of our country, and in that city Congress has met ever since.

I must say something here about another of the great men of Revolutionary times, Alexander Hamilton. He was great in financial or money matters, and this was very important at that time, for the finances of the country were in a sad state.

In the Revolution our people had very little money, and that was one reason why they had so much suffering. Congress soon ran out of gold and silver, so it issued paper money. This did very well for a time, and in the end, a great deal of paper money was set afloat, but people soon began to get afraid of it. There was too much money of this kind for so poor a country. The value of the Continental currency, as it was called, began to go down, and the price of everything else to go up. In time, the paper money lost almost all its value.

Such was the money the people had at the end of the Revolution. It was not good for much, was it? But it was the only kind of money Congress had to pay the soldiers with or to pay the other debts of the government. The country owed much more money than it could pay, so that it was what we call bankrupt. Nobody would trust it or take its paper in payment. What Alexander Hamilton did was to help the country to pay its debts and to bring back its lost credit, and in that way he won great honor.

Hamilton came to this country from the West Indies during the Revolution. He was then only a boy, but he soon showed himself a good soldier, and Washington made him an officer on his staff and one of his friends. He often asked young Hamilton for advice, and took it, too.

Hamilton was one of the men who made the Constitution, and when Washington became President, he chose him as his Secretary of the Treasury. That is, he gave him the money affairs of the government to look after. Hamilton was not afraid of the load of debt, and he soon took off its weight. He asked Congress to pay not only its own debt, but that of the States as well, and also to make good all the paper money. Congress did not like to do this, but Hamilton talked to the members till he got them to do so.

Then he set himself to pay it. He laid a tax on whiskey and brandy and on all goods that came into the country. He had a mint and a national bank built in Philadelphia. He made the debt a government fund, or loan, on which he agreed to pay interest and to pay off the principal as fast as possible. It was not long before all the fund was taken up by those who had money, and the country got back its lost credit. After that, all went well.

Washington was President for eight years. That made two terms of four years each. Many wished to make him President for a third term, but he refused to run again.

George Washington had done enough for his country. He loved his home, but he had little time to live there. When he was only a boy, he was called away to take part in the French and Indian War. Then, after spending some happy years at home, he was called away again to lead the army in the Revolutionary War. Finally, he served his country eight years as President.

He was now growing old and wanted rest, and he went back with joy to his beloved home at Mount Vernon, hoping to spend there the remainder of his days. But trouble arose with France, and it looked as if there would be a new war, and Washington was asked to take command of the army again. He consented, though he had had enough of fighting; but fortunately the war did not come, so he was not obliged to abandon his home.

He died in December, 1799, near the end of the century of which he was one of the greatest men. The news of his death filled all American hearts with grief. Not while the United States exists will the name of Washington be forgotten or left without honor. His home and tomb at Mt. Vernon are visited each year by thousands of patriotic Americans. As was said of him long ago by General Henry Lee, he was and is, "first in war, first in peace, and first in the hearts of his countrymen."

Chapter 25
America Grows

I wonder if any of my young readers are curious to know who became President after George Washington served his two terms so capably and so well. As you have heard, a great many able and noble men led our country through the Revolution, and many of them also led our country as President in their turns. I shall tell you about two of them now.

When George Washington returned to his beloved Mount Vernon, the people elected John Adams to be their next President. It was during his term of service that the seat of government moved to the capital city of Washington, where it has remained ever since. John Adams packed up his belongings and moved into the newly built White House, though it was not finished yet. It had no carpet on the floors and many rooms were still incomplete. Laundry was hung from a clothesline along the East Room wall.

On his second day in the house Adams wrote a letter to his wife Abigail, closing with the words: "I pray Heaven to bestow the best of blessings on this House, and all that shall hereafter inhabit it. May none but honest and wise men ever rule under this roof." Do you not think that a beautiful prayer? It has since been engraved in a fireplace mantel so that, throughout the years, all who walk the halls of this great House can read it and remember what an honorable responsibility it is to serve as President of the United States.

After John Adams, the people elected another Revolutionary patriot to be president. That was Thomas Jefferson. I am sure you remember that he wrote the Declaration of Independence. Well, during his presidency, Jefferson had the happy opportunity to purchase a large portion of land from France. You see, all the land west of the Mississippi River belonged to France. The Louisiana Territory they called it, after their king, Louis XIV. Napoleon Bonaparte, who was then the emperor of France, was asked to sell New Orleans to the United States, for they wished their vessels to go down the Mississippi to the sea without sailing through land held by Spain or France. Napoleon was then at war with England and other countries, and did not care a fig for all the wild land beyond the seas. What he wanted was money to buy food and arms for his soldiers. So he offered to sell, not only New Orleans, but the whole vast country of Louisiana to the United States for fifteen million dollars. That amount seems very high until you realize the number of acres it purchased—millions of acres, and each acre cost only three cents! Thomas Jefferson agreed to buy that great region, and by a stroke of the pen it became part of the United States.

Imagine if behind your house were a large piece of land that you had never set foot on and you suddenly had the opportunity to buy it. What would you do after the purchase? I fancy you would set out to explore your new territory. And that is just what President Jefferson did. He sent out an exploring party of about fifty brave men, led by his friend, Meriwether Lewis, and another bold man, William Clark.

Their plan was to launch their journey of discovery near St. Louis and travel up the Missouri River as far as they could. Then they would see if they could track through the uncharted lands all the way to the west coast of the continent and the Pacific Ocean. Along the way they would gather information and record what they saw, so those living in the United States would have a good idea of what kind of territory they had just purchased.

Clark's job was to gather measurements and note what the land was like across the miles, so he could make an accurate map of it. Lewis wrote descriptions and drew detailed sketches of the plants and animals that they saw during their journey. As they traveled, they saw the landscape change from dense forest to open grasslands to snow-capped mountains. The animals were different too, and Lewis took careful notes of all he saw. The team even sent a live magpie and a prairie dog back to the White House for the astounded President Jefferson to observe in person.

Indians lived all along the explorers' route. Some of these Indians were friendly and they welcomed the group of explorers; others were troublesome, especially a tribe called the Lakotas. These unfriendly Indians stole horses and sent false warnings to other tribes, telling lies about Lewis and Clark and stirring up all kinds of trouble.

After six months of difficult and perilous journeying, the team came to the end of their current map. Everything ahead of them was now unknown territory. What might they find around the next bend? They knew not. But winter was coming on quickly, so our brave explorers stopped to wait out the bad weather.

They built their winter fort near a large Mandan Indian settlement. Now it happened that in this large encampment several Indians from other tribes lived with the Mandans. And it further happened that one day Lewis found a Shoshone Indian girl named Sacagawea living there. The explorers decided to hire her and her husband to come with them. They had been told that farther downstream they would meet the Shoshone tribe, and they thought Sacagawea could interpret for them since she knew that Indian language.

In April, when the weather turned warmer, Lewis and Clark and their team of discoverers launched their boats and headed west again. Soon they heard a constant and mysterious roar in the distance and saw what looked like columns of smoke rising from the river ahead. As they got closer, they discovered that the roar of noise and mysterious spray was created by a waterfall, ascending eighty feet into the air before them. There was nothing for it but to pull the boats out of the water and carry the heavy, awkward vessels, along with all their supplies, through the brush and rocks, up the steep climb, and around the cascading water. It was tough going. Biting mosquitoes and buzzing gnats swarmed the travelers, now that they were advancing much slower on foot. Prickly cactuses poked through the men's worn moccasins as they trudged along, hauling their burdens up the incline. And just when they thought they had accomplished their task, they discovered another waterfall ahead, and another. Within ten miles, there were four waterfalls, and they would have to portage around all of them the same way. It took nearly a month, but they heroically kept going amid the heat and blisters, and they made it around those waterfalls!

Along the journey, the team came across little creeks, rivers, or other landmarks and decided to think of names for them. I wonder what name you would give a new river or mountain that you discovered. Well, these men gave them names like Marias River, which was named after one man's cousin who lived in Virginia, and Council Bluff, to commemorate where the captains met for a council with some Indian chiefs. Of course, the two captains named two of the rivers in honor of each other, the Lewis River and Clark's River.

They even named a creek after Lewis' Newfoundland dog, Seaman. This faithful, shaggy companion proved his worth many times on the journey. He once saved the lives of the explorers by barking at a stampeding buffalo bull to scare it away, and as they traveled deeper into the wilderness, he patrolled the camp all night, on the alert for bears. Once, an Indian offered three beaver skins in trade for the dog, but Lewis wouldn't think of letting him go. And when three Indians tried to steal Seaman, the explorers gave chase and got the dog back.

Seaman was with them when the team of explorers finally

came to the foot of the majestic Rocky Mountains. There the group found the Shoshone tribe of Indians, just as they had hoped. Lewis and Clark knew that their big, heavy boats would be useless in crossing the Rockies. They needed horses to carry them over the towering mountains and explore the territory that they would find on the other side. So they asked the Shoshones to provide them with horses for the journey ahead. But the Shoshones were suspicious that these strange white men had been sent by an enemy Indian tribe to try to steal their horses, and they were reluctant to do business. As the men gathered with the Shoshones to discuss the matter, they called for Sacagawea to interpret this important meeting for them. No sooner had Sacagawea sat down when she instantly jumped up again. She ran to the Shoshone chief and embraced him, weeping with joy. The chief was her brother!

Of course, the Shoshones trusted the exploration team after that. The discoverers easily got the horses they needed and began the perilous climb over the Rocky Mountains. You must remember that there were no roads over the Mountains when Lewis and Clark's band of men crossed them. They had to pick their way through the sliding rocks and steep ledges, covered with snow and ice, and try to find the best route up and over that they could. It was a dangerous crossing. And to make matters worse, the men's food ran out when they were only part of the way over. But still they struggled on, hungry, weak, and cold.

At the bottom of the mountain they discovered two important things that renewed their courage. The first thing they discovered was another tribe of Indians, the Nimipu. These kind Indians fed the men salmon and helped them regain their strength so they could finish their journey. And the Nimipu also showed them the second important thing: a river that was headed toward the Pacific Ocean, the Columbia River. With the Indians' help, the explorers cut down pine trees and made new canoes to carry them down the river and toward the sea. They were almost there!

As they paddled down the Columbia river, they saw signs that they were getting near the ocean. Ducks, geese, and gulls were everywhere. In fact, the raucous noise from these great flocks kept Lewis awake at night. The river widened and the weather grew damp. The water grew salty, too salty to drink. The men depended on rain water to quench their thirst as they labored to complete their assignment.

And complete it they did! When they reached the vast Pacific Ocean, these brave and bold men had blazed a trail of more than 4,000 miles. After two and a half years of traveling, Lewis and Clark and their daring companions returned to St. Louis, carrying with them valuable discoveries about the new territory that was now part of the United States of America.

Chapter 26
The Steamboat and the Cotton Gin

I think you must now have learned a great deal about the history of your country from the time Columbus crossed the ocean till the year 1800. You have been told about discovery, and settlement, and wars, and modes of life, and government, and other things, but you must bear in mind that these are not the whole of history. The story of our country is broad and deep enough to hold many other things than these. For instance, there is the story of our great inventors, to whom we owe so much. I propose in this chapter to tell you about some of those who lived near the year 1800.

First, I must ask you to go back with me to a kitchen in Scotland many years ago. On the open hearth of that kitchen a bright fire blazed, and nearby sat a thoughtful-faced boy, with his eyes fixed on the tea-kettle which was boiling away over the fire, while its lid kept lifting to let the steam escape. His mother, who was hustling about, no doubt thought him idle, and may have scolded him a little. But he was far from idle; he was busy at work—not with his hands, but with his brain. The brain, you know, may be hard at work while the body is doing nothing.

How many of you have seen the lid of a kettle of boiling water keeping up its clatter as the steam lifts it and puffs out into the air? And what thought has this brought into your mind? Into the mind of little James Watt, the Scotch boy, it brought one great thought, that of power. As he looked at it, he said to himself that the steam which comes from boiling water must have a great deal of force, if a little of it could keep the kettle lid clattering up and down; and he asked himself if such a power could not be put to some good use.

Our Scotch boy was not the first one to have that thought. Others had thought the same thing, and steam had been used to move a poor sort of engine. But what James Watt did when he grew up, was to invent a much better engine than had ever been made before. It was a great day when that steam engine was invented. Before that time, men had done most of the work of the world with their hands, and you may imagine that the work went on very slowly. After that time, much of the world's work was done with the aid of the steam engine, and one man could do as much as many men could have done in the past.

Now let us come back to our American inventors. I have spoken about the steam engine because it was with this that most of them worked. They thought that if horses could drag a wagon over the ground and the wind could drive a vessel through the water, steam might do the same thing, and they set themselves to see in what way a carriage or a boat could be moved by a steam engine.

Very likely you have all heard about Robert Fulton and his steamboat, but you may not know that steamboats were running on American waters years before that of Fulton was built. Why, as long ago as 1768, before the Revolutionary War, Oliver Evans, one of our first inventors, had made a little boat which was moved by steam and paddle-wheels. Years afterwards he made a large engine for a boat at New Orleans. It was put in the boat, but there came a dry season and low water, so that the boat could not be used, and the owners took the engine out and set it to work on a saw-mill. It did so well there that it was never put back in the boat; so that steamboat never had a chance.

Oliver Evans was the first man who lived to make a steam-carriage, but there were others who thought they could move a boat by steam. Some of these were in Europe and some in America. Down in Virginia was an inventor named Rumsey who moved a boat at the speed of four miles an hour. In this boat jets of water were pumped through the stern and forced the boat along. In Philadelphia was another man named John Fitch, who was the first man to make a successful steamboat. His boat was moved with paddles like an Indian canoe. It was put on the Delaware River, between Philadelphia and Trenton in 1790, and ran for several months as a passenger boat, at the speed of seven or eight miles an hour. Poor John Fitch! He was unfortunate and in the end he killed himself.

I am glad to be able to tell you a different story of the next man who tried to make a steamboat. His name was Robert Fulton. He was born in Pennsylvania, and as a boy was very fond of the water, he and the other boys having an old flat-boat which they pushed along with a pole. Fulton got tired of this way of getting along, and like a natural-born inventor, set his wits to work. In the end he made two paddle wheels which hung over the sides and could be moved in the water by turning a crank and so force the boat onward. The boys found this much easier than the pole, and likely enough young Fulton thought a large vessel might be moved in the same way.

He knew all about what others had done. He had heard how Rumsey moved his boat by pumping water through the stern, and Fitch by paddling it along. And he had seen a boat in Scotland moved by a stern paddle-wheel. I fancy he had not forgotten the side paddle-wheel he made as a boy to go fishing with, for when he set out to invent his steamboat, this is the plan he tried.

Fulton made his first boat in France, but things didn't work out for him there. Then he came to America and built a boat in New York. While he was at work on this boat in America, James Watt, of whom I have already told you, was building him an engine in England. He wanted the best engine that he could get, and he thought the Scotch inventor was the right man to make it.

While Fulton was working, some of the smart New Yorkers were laughing. They called his boat "Fulton's Folly," and said it would not move faster than the tide would carry it. But he let them laugh and worked on, and at last, one day in 1807, the new boat, which he named the *Clermont,* was afloat in the Hudson ready for trial. Hundreds of curious people came to see it start. Some were ready to laugh again when they saw the boat, with its clumsy paddle-wheels hanging down in the water on both sides. They were not covered with wooden frames as were such wheels afterwards.

"That boat move? So will a log move if set adrift," said the wiseacres. "It will move when the tide moves it, and not before." But none of them felt like laughing when they saw the wheels begin to turn and the boat to glide out into the stream, moving against the tide.

"She moves! she moves!" cried the crowd, and nobody said a word about "Fulton's Folly."

Move she did. Up the Hudson she went against wind and current, and reached Albany, one hundred and forty-two miles away, in thirty-two hours. This was at the rate of four and a half miles an hour. It was not many years before steamboats were running on all our rivers.

That is all I shall say here about the steamboat, for there is another story of invention I wish to tell you before I close. This is about cotton, which you know is a great product of the Southern States.

The cotton plant, when ripe, has a white, fluffy head, a great bunch of snow-white fibers within, which are intermixed with the seeds. In old times these had to be taken out by hand, and it was a whole day's work for a man to get the seeds out of a pound of cotton. This made cotton so dear that not much of it could be sold. In 1784 eight bags of it were sent to Liverpool, and the custom-house people there seized it for duties. They said it must have been smuggled from some other country, for the United States could not have produced such a "prodigious quantity."

A few years afterwards, a young man named Eli Whitney went South to teach in a private family, but before he got there someone else took the job, and he was left with nothing to do. Mrs. Greene, the widow of General Greene who fought so well in the Revolution, took pity on him and gave him a home in her house. He paid her by fixing up things about her house. She found him so handy that she asked him if he could not invent a machine to take the seeds out of the cotton. Whitney said he would try, and he set himself to work. It was not long before he had a machine made which did the work wonderfully well. This machine is known as the "cotton-gin," or cotton engine, for gin is short for engine. On one side of it are wires so close together that the seeds cannot get through. Between them are circular saws which catch the cotton and draw it through, while the seeds pass on.

The machine was a simple one, but it acted like magic. A hundred men could not clean as much cotton in a day as one machine. The price of cotton soon went down and a demand for it sprang up. In 1795, when the cotton gin was made, only about 500,000 pounds of cotton were produced in this country. By 1801, only six years later, production had grown to 20 million pounds.

New England Boy's Song about Thanksgiving Day

Lydia Maria Child

Over the river and through the wood,
To grandfather's house we go;
 The horse knows the way
 To carry the sleigh
Through the white and drifted snow.

Over the river and through the wood—
Oh, how the wind does blow!
 It stings the toes
 And bites the nose,
As over the ground we go.

Over the river and through the wood,
To have a first-rate play.
 Hear the bells ring,
 "Ting-a-ling-ding!"
Hurrah for Thanksgiving Day!

Over the river and through the wood
Trot fast, my dapple-gray!

Spring over the ground,
Like a hunting hound!
For this is Thanksgiving Day!

Over the river and through the wood,
And straight through the barn-yard gate.
    We seem to go
    Extremely slow,—
It is so hard to wait!

Over the river and through the wood—
Now grandmother's cap I spy!
    Hurrah for the fun!
    Is the pudding done?
Hurrah for the pumpkin-pie!

Chapter 27

How the English and the Americans Fought Again

For years before and after the year 1800 all Europe was filled with war and bloodshed. I have mentioned Napoleon Bonaparte before. He was one of the greatest generals that ever lived, and one of the most cruel men. Napoleon was at the head of the armies of France, and was fighting all Europe. England was his greatest enemy and fought him on land and sea, and this fighting on the sea made trouble between England and the United States.

The English wanted men for their war-vessels and said they had a right to take Englishmen wherever they could find them. So they began to take sailors off of American merchant vessels. They said that these men were deserters from the British navy, but the fact is that many of them were true-born Americans, and our people grew very angry as this went on year after year.

What made it worse was the insolence of some of the British captains. One of them went so far as to stop an American war-vessel, the *Chesapeake,* and demand part of her crew, who, he said, were British deserters. When Captain Barron refused to give them up, the British captain fired all his guns and killed and wounded numbers of the American crew. The *Chesapeake* had no guns fit to fire back, so her flag had to be pulled down and the men to be given up.

You may well imagine that this insult made the American

blood boil. There would have been war at that time if the British government had not apologized and offered to pay for the injury. A few years afterwards the insult was paid for in a different way. Another proud British captain thought he could treat Americans in the same insulting fashion. The frigate *President* met the British sloop-of-war *Little Belt,* and hailed it, the captain calling through his trumpet, "What ship is that?"

Instead of giving a civil reply, the British captain answered with a cannon shot. Then the *President* fired a broadside which killed eleven and wounded twenty-one men on the *Little Belt.* When the captain of the *President* hailed again, the insolent Briton was glad to reply in a more civil fashion. He had been taught a useful lesson.

The United States was then a poor country, and not in condition to go to war. But no nation could submit to such insults as these. It is said that more than six thousand sailors had been taken from our merchant ships, and among these were two nephews of George Washington, who were seized while they were on their way home from Europe, and put to work as common seamen on a British war-vessel.

At length, on June 18, 1812, the United States declared war against Great Britain. It had put up with insults and injuries as long as it could bear them. It did not take long to teach the haughty British captains that American sea-dogs were not to be played with. The little American fleet put to sea, and before the end of the year it had captured no less than five of the best ships in the British navy and had not lost a single ship in return. I fancy the people of England quit singing their proud song, "Britannia rules the waves."

Shall I tell you the whole story of this war? I do not think it worth while, for there is much of it you would not care to hear. The war went on for two years and a half, on sea and land, but there were not many important battles and the United States did not win much honor on land. But on the sea the sailors of our country covered themselves with glory.

Most of the land battles were along the borders of Canada. Here there was a good deal of fighting, but most of it was of no great account. At first the British had the best of it, and then the Americans began to win battles, but it all came to an end about where it began. Neither side gained anything for the men that were killed.

There was one naval battle in the north that I must tell you about. On Lake Erie the British had a fleet of six war-vessels, and for a time they had everything their own way. Then Captain Oliver Perry, a young officer, was sent to the lake to build a fleet and fight the British.

When he got there his ships were growing in the woods. He had to cut down trees and build ships from their timber. But he worked like a young giant, and in a few weeks he had some vessels built and afloat. He got others on the lake, and in a wonderfully short time he had a fleet on the lake and was sailing out to find the British ships.

They met on September 10, 1813. The Americans had the most vessels, but the British had the most guns, and soon they were fighting like sea-dragons. The *Lawrence,* Captain Perry's flag-ship, fought two of the largest British ships till it was nearly ready to sink, and so many of its crew were killed and wounded that it had only eight men left fit for fighting. What do you think brave Perry did then? He leaped into a small boat and was rowed away, with the American flag floating in his hand, though the British ships were firing hotly at him.

When he reached the *Niagara,* another of his ships, he sprang on board and sailed right through the enemy's fleet, firing right and left into their shattered vessels. The British soon had enough of this, and in fifteen minutes more they gave up the fight.

"We have met the enemy and they are ours," wrote Perry to General Harrison. He was a born hero of the waves.

Now I think we had better take a look out to sea and learn what was going on there. We did not have many ships, but they were like so many bulldogs in a flock of sheep. The whole world looked on with surprise to see our little fleet of war-vessels making such havoc in the proud British navy, which no country in Europe had ever been able to defeat.

In less than two months after war was declared, the frigate *Essex* met the British sloop-of-war *Alert* and took it in eight minutes, without losing a man. The *Essex* was too strong for the *Alert,* but six days afterwards the *Constitution* met the *Guerriere,* and these vessels were nearly the same in size. But in half an hour the *Guerriere* was nearly cut to pieces and ready to sink, and had lost a hundred of her men. The others were hastily taken off, and then down went the proud British frigate to the bottom of the Gulf of St. Lawrence.

All the island of Great Britain went into mourning when it learned how the Americans had served this good ship. There was soon more to mourn for. The American sloop *Wasp* captured the British sloop *Frolic.* The frigate *United States* captured the frigate *Macedonia.* The *Constitution* met the *Java* and served it the same way as it had done the *Guerriere.* In two hours the *Java* was a wreck. Soon after, the sloop *Hornet* met the ship *Peacock* and handled her so severely that she sank while the crew was being taken off.

Later on the British won two battles at sea, and that was all they gained during the whole war. On the water the honors stayed with the Americans.

There was one affair in which the British won dishonor instead of honor. In July, 1814, a strong British fleet sailed up Chesapeake Bay, with an army of nearly five thousand men on board. These were landed and marched on the city of Washington, the capital of the young republic.

Their coming was a surprise. There were few trained soldiers to meet this army, and those were not the days of railroads, so no troops could be brought in haste from afar. Those that gathered were nearly all raw militia, and they did not stand long before the British veterans who had fought in the wars with Napoleon. They were soon put to flight and the British army marched into our capital city.

There they behaved in a way that their country has ever since been ashamed of. They set fire to the public buildings and burned most of them to the ground. The Capitol, the President's house, and other buildings were burned, and the records of the government were destroyed. Then, having acted like so many savages, the British hurried away before the Americans could get at them for revenge. That was a victory, I fancy, which the British do not like to read about.

They had been so successful at Washington that they thought they would try the same thing with another city. This time they picked out New Orleans, which was so far away from the thickly settled part of the country that they fancied it would be an easy matter to capture it. In this they made a great mistake, as you will soon see.

There was a general at New Orleans who was not used to being defeated. His name was Andrew Jackson, one of our bravest soldiers. He also had won fame in the war he waged with the Indians in Florida. He was a man who was always ready to fight, and this the English found when they marched on New Orleans. There were twelve thousand of them, and Jackson only had half that many. And the British were trained soldiers, while the Americans were militia. But they were old hunters and knew how to shoot.

Some of you may have heard that Jackson's men fought behind cotton bales. That is not quite true, but he was in such a hurry in building his breastworks that he did put in them some bales of cotton taken from the warehouses. The British, who were in as great a hurry, built a breastwork of sugar barrels which they found on the plantations. But the cannonballs soon set the cotton on fire and filled the air with flying sugar, so the bales and the barrels had to be pulled out. It was found that cotton and sugar, while good enough in their place, were not good things to stop cannonballs.

Soon the British marched against the American works and there was a terrible fight.

"Stand to your guns, my men," said Jackson to his soldiers. "Make every shot tell. Give it to them."

Many of the men were old hunters from Tennessee, some of whom could hit a squirrel in the eye, and when they fired, the British fell in rows. Not a man could cross that terrible wall of fire, and they fought on until twenty-six hundred of the British lay bleeding on the field, while only eight Americans were killed.

That ended the battle. It ended the war also, and it was the last time Americans and Englishmen ever fought with each other. Jackson became the hero of the country, and he was finally elected President of the United States. I cannot say that he was a very good President. He was a very obstinate man, who always wanted to have his own way, and that is better in a soldier than in a president.

Chapter 28
Our National Anthem

Do you know any songs that tell a story? Many songs do. And there is an important story-song that came out of the War of 1812, of which I have just told you. It is such an important story-song, that whenever it is played or sung, Americans will rise to their feet to show their respect. Men and boys will remove their hats, and people will often place their hands upon their hearts as a demonstration of their love and loyalty. That song is The Star-Spangled Banner, and I shall tell you its story.

It is a story of two men: a doctor and a lawyer. The doctor, Dr. Beanes, had served in the Revolutionary War and was deeply saddened when the United States declared war on England again. He had seen too many good men die on the battlefield to ever welcome war with any country. His lawyer friend, Francis Scott Key, had a law practice near Washington, D. C. In fact, Key's house was close enough to Washington that he saw the city go up in flames when the British set it on fire and destroyed all those government records.

Well, one day a friend rushed to Key's house and breathlessly informed him that the British had arrested Dr. Beanes. He had been accused of a false charge and taken prisoner on board their flagship in the Chesapeake. If Key went onboard the British ship, he might be able to plead Dr. Beanes's case and secure his safe release.

Key rushed to help. He traveled to Baltimore to be near the British fleet where Dr. Beanes was being held. Then he sailed out of Baltimore on an American ship named the *Minden,* in search of the British flagship. As the *Minden* left its port, it passed by Fort McHenry, a strong fort shaped like a star, which stood at the entrance to the Baltimore harbor to defend the city. Everyone in the fort was on the alert, for the British fleet was near and a fight seemed imminent. Over the fort flew the largest American flag that Francis Scott Key had ever seen. It measured thirty feet by forty-two feet and had been lovingly stitched by a young widow, Mrs. Pickersgill. I wonder if my young readers can imagine a flag so large that it was as tall as a three-story house! The enemy could certainly see a banner that large from a long distance!

The *Minden* soon found the British fleet nearby, and the captain of the British flagship allowed Key to come aboard to defend Dr. Beanes. He listened carefully to Key's arguments that Dr. Beanes was not a threat to the British, that he was a peace-loving man who only wanted to help the sick and wounded. Key also gave the captain letters from many American soldiers, testifying that Dr. Beanes had treated their wounds and was a good man.

As Key presented his case, he noticed a lot of bustling about on the British ship. Sailors were moving briskly with quick, alert eyes, but hardly seemed to notice that an American was on board. Finally, the captain agreed to dismiss the charges against Dr. Beanes and return him to the *Minden.* However, now it came to light that they were preparing to attack Fort McHenry that very day, and they would not let Key and Beanes's ship leave until the attack was over. They were returned to their ship, the *Minden,* but with a British crew in charge to make sure they did not sail for Baltimore.

How frustrating to sit amongst the enemy's ships and watch them bombard the American shores! But there was nothing Key nor Dr. Beanes could do. Anxiously they kept their eyes on that huge American flag flying over Fort McHenry. If the British took the fort, that flag would come down. But as long as it was flying, they would know that Baltimore was safe and the American soldiers were winning the battle.

Soon choking smoke settled over the waters, and Key and Dr. Beanes could scarcely see the fort or the flag. Night came on, and with it, rain clouds that blotted out the moon. Now Key could see the flag only when a bomb burst and lit up the night sky. All that terrible night he wondered if the Americans could hold the fort. He wondered if the flag would still be flying when dawn's light broke upon the waters.

As he paced the deck, wondering and watching, Key took an envelope out of his pocket and jotted down words and phrases that described what he was seeing and feeling.

At dawn's early light, two joyful men beheld the oversized star-spangled banner still flying over Fort McHenry. The Americans had won the battle! The flag was still flying! The British crew left the *Minden,* as agreed, and the defeated British fleet sailed away.

When Key and Beanes arrived back in town, Key took the phrases he had jotted down on the envelope and composed a poem about the experience.

O say, can you see, by the dawn's early light,
What so proudly we hailed at the twilight's last gleaming?
Whose broad stripes and bright stars, through the perilous fight,
O'er the ramparts we watched were so gallantly streaming!
And the rockets' red glare, the bombs bursting in air,
Gave proof through the night that our flag was still there:
O say, does that star-spangled banner yet wave
O'er the land of the free and the home of the brave?

On the shore, dimly seen through the mists of the deep,
Where the foe's haughty host in dread silence reposes,
What is that which the breeze, o'er the towering steep,
As it fitfully blows, half conceals, half discloses?

Now it catches the gleam of the morning's first beam,
In full glory reflected now shines on the stream.
'Tis the star-spangled banner! O long may it wave
O'er the land of the free and the home of the brave!

And where is that band who so vauntingly swore
That the havoc of war and the battle's confusion
A home and a country should leave us no more?
Their blood has washed out their foul footsteps' pollution.
No refuge could save the hireling and slave
From the terror of flight, or the gloom of the grave:
And the star-spangled banner in triumph doth wave
O'er the land of the free and the home of the brave!

O thus be it ever, when freemen shall stand
Between their loved homes and the war's desolation!
Blest with victory and peace, may the heaven-rescued land
Praise the Power that hath made and preserved us a nation.
Then conquer we must, when our cause it is just,
And this be our motto: "In God is our trust,"
And the star-spangled banner in triumph shall wave
O'er the land of the free and the home of the brave!

Newspapers printed the patriotic poem and it quickly spread across the nation. Soon everyone was singing the words set to an old hymn tune, and it has endured ever since. More than one hundred years after the battle of Fort McHenry, in 1931, President Hoover signed a congressional resolution making *The Star-Spangled Banner* our national anthem.

Chapter 29

Remember the Alamo

I have told you the story of more than one war. I shall have to tell you now about still another in which the Americans fought the Mexicans in Texas.

I suppose you know that Texas is one of our largest States. In former times it was part of Mexico, and was a portion of what is called Spanish America. But there got to be more Americans in it than there were Spanish. People kept coming there from the United States until it was much more of an American than a Spanish country.

General Santa Anna, who was at the head of the Mexican government at the time I speak of, was a good deal of a tyrant, and he tried to rule the people of Texas in a way they would not submit to. Then he ordered them to give up all their guns to his soldiers, but instead of that, they took their guns and drove the Mexican soldiers away. After that there was war, as you might well suppose.

I wish now to tell you about what happened to some very brave Americans. There were only one hundred and seventy-five of them, and they were attacked by General Santa Anna with an army of several thousand men. But they were commanded by Colonel Travis, a brave young Texan, and among them was the famous David Crockett, a great hunter, and Colonel James Bowie, who invented the terrible "bowie-knife," and other bold and daring men. They had made a fort of an old Spanish building called the Alamo.

The kind of men I have named do not easily give up. The Mexicans poured bomb-shells and cannonballs into their fort, battering down the walls and killing many of them, but they fought on like tigers, determined to die rather than surrender. At length so many of them were dead that there were not enough left to defend the walls, and the Mexican soldiers captured the Alamo. The valiant Crockett kept on fighting, and when he fell, the ground before him was covered with Mexican dead. Then Santa Anna ordered his soldiers to shoot down all that were left. That is what is called the "Massacre of the Alamo."

It was not long before the Americans had their revenge. Their principal leader was a bold and able man named Samuel Houston. He had less than eight hundred men under him, but he marched on the Mexicans, who had then about eighteen hundred men.

"Men, there is the enemy," said brave General Houston. "Do you wish to fight?"

"We do," they all shouted.

"Charge on them, then, for liberty or death! Remember the Alamo!"

"Remember the Alamo!" they cried, as they rushed onward with the courage of lions.

In a little time the Mexicans were running like frightened deer, and the daring Texans were like deer hounds on their track. Of the eighteen hundred Mexicans, all but four hundred were killed, wounded, or taken prisoners, while the Americans lost only thirty men. They had well avenged the gallant Travis and his men.

The cruel Santa Anna was taken prisoner. Many of the Texans wanted to hang him for his murders at the Alamo, but in the end he was set free.

All this took place in 1835. Texas was made an independent country, the "Lone Star Republic," with General Houston for President. But its people did not want to stand alone. They were

American born and wished to belong to the United States. So this country was asked to accept Texas as a State of the Union. Nine years after, this was done.

Perhaps some of my readers may think that this story has much more to do with the history of Mexico than that of the United States. But the taking of Texas as a State was United States history, and so was what followed. You know how one thing leads to another. Mexico did not feel like giving up Texas so easily, and her rulers said that the United States had no right to take it. It was not long before the soldiers of the two countries met on the border lands and blood was shed. There was a sharp fight at a place called Palo Alto and a sharper one at a place called Resaca de la Palma. In both of them the Mexicans were defeated.

Congress then declared war against Mexico, and very soon there was hard fighting going on elsewhere. General Zachary Taylor, a brave officer, who had fought the Seminole Indians in Florida, led the American troops across the Rio Grande River into Mexico, and some time afterwards marched to a place called Buena Vista. He had only five thousand men, while Santa Anna was marching against him with twenty thousand—four to one. General Taylor's army was in great danger. Santa Anna sent him a message, asking him to surrender if he did not want his army to be cut to pieces; but Rough and Ready, as Taylor's men called him, sent word back that he was there to fight, not to surrender.

The battle that followed was a desperate one. It took place on February 23, 1847. The Mexican lancers rode bravely against the American lines and were driven back at the cannon's mouth. For ten long hours the fighting went on. The Mexicans gained the high ground above the pass and put the American troops in danger. Charge after charge was made, but like bull dogs the Yankee soldiers held their ground. On came the dashing Mexican lancers, shouting their war-cry of "God and Liberty," and charging a battery commanded by Captain Bragg. The lancers captured some of the guns and drove the soldiers back. Captain Bragg sent a messenger in haste to General Taylor, saying that he must have more men.

"I have no more men to send you," said Rough and Ready. "Give them a little more grape, Captain Bragg."

The cannon were loaded with grape-shot and fired into the ranks of the enemy, cutting great gaps through them. Again and again they were loaded and fired, and then the fine Mexican cavalry turned and fled. They could not stand any more of Captain Bragg's grape.

That night both armies went to sleep on the field of battle. But when the next day dawned, the Mexicans were gone. Santa Anna had led them away during the night and General Taylor had won the greatest victory of the war. He received a noble reward for it, for the following year he was elected President of the United States.

The next thing done in this war was an attempt to capture the city of Mexico, the capital of the country. The easiest way to get there was by sea, for it was a long journey by land, so a fleet was got ready and an army sent south on the Gulf of Mexico. This army was led by General Winfield Scott, who had fought against the British in the War of 1812.

Onward they sailed till they came before the seaport city of Vera Cruz. This had a strong fort, which was battered for four days by the American cannon, when its walls were so shattered that the Mexicans gave it up. In this way a good starting-point was gained.

But I would have you all know that the Americans had no easy road before them. The city of Mexico lies in the center of the country on land that is as high as many mountains, and the way to it from the coast goes steadily upward, and has many difficult passes and rough places, where a small force might stop an army.

If the Mexicans had known their business and had possessed good generals, I am afraid the Americans might never have got up this rugged road. The Mexicans had men enough, but they wanted able leaders. At one of the passes, named Cerro Gordo, Santa

Anna waited with 15,000 men. The Americans had only 9,000. It looked as if they might have to turn back.

What did they do? Why, they managed to drag a battery to the top of a steep hill that overlooked the pass. And while these guns poured their shot down on the astonished Mexicans, the army attacked them in front. In a few hours they were in full flight. Five generals and 3,000 men were taken prisoners, and Santa Anna himself came so near being taken that he left his cork leg behind.

Onward they marched until not very far away lay the beautiful city of Mexico. But here and there along the road were strong forts, and Santa Anna had collected a large army, three times as large as that of the Americans. You may see that General Scott had a very hard task before him. But here is one way to get past forts without fighting; which is, to go around them. This is what General Scott did. He marched to the south, and soon he was within ten miles of the capital without a battle.

August 20th was a great day for the American army. That day our brave troops fought like heroes, and before night they had won five victories. One of these was on a steep hill called Churubusco, which they charged up in the face of the Mexican guns. Then on they went, and in a short time more the old city, the most ancient in America, was in their hands. That ended the war. When peace was made, the United States claimed the provinces of New Mexico and California, which had been captured by our soldiers, but for which Mexico was paid a large sum. No one then dreamed how rich those provinces were in silver and gold.

Helpful
Maps

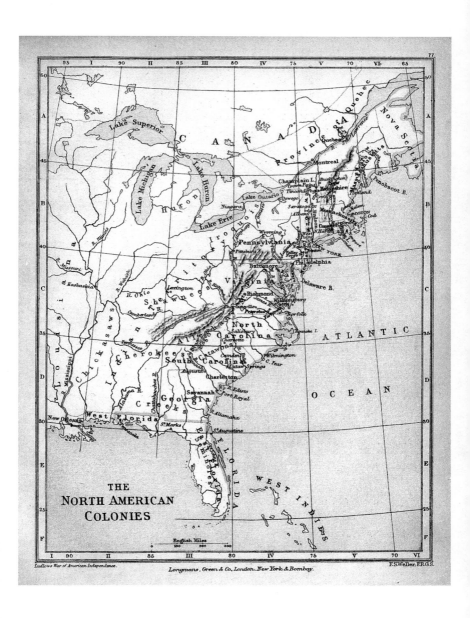

THE
NORTH AMERICAN
COLONIES

English Miles

Ludlow's War of American Independence.

Longmans, Green & Co., London, New York & Bombay.

F.S.Weller, F.R.G.S.

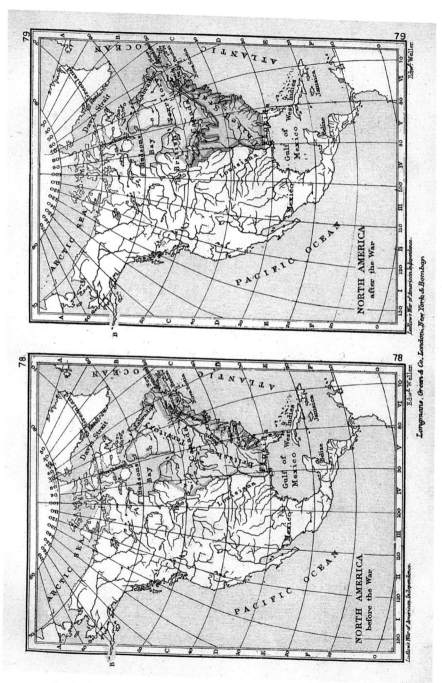